Proceedings of The National Ballet of Canada's 25th Anniversary Conference, held in Toronto, 15-16 November, 1976.

VISIONS

Foreword by Sir Frederick Ashton
Introduction by Vincent Tovell

VISIONS

BALLET AND ITS FUTURE

Michael Crabb, Editor

**Essays from the International Dance Conference
to commemorate the 25th anniversary of
The National Ballet of Canada**

Simon & Pierre
TORONTO

ISBN 0-88924-079-5
5 4 3 2 1 • 3 2 1 0 9

Simon & Pierre Publishing Company Limited
Order Department: P.O. Box 280, Adelaide Street Postal Station
Toronto, Ontario, Canada M5C 2J4

Assistant Editor: Holly Small
Printer: The Hunter Rose Company
Designer: Garfield Reeves-Stevens/First Image

Copy Editor: Jennifer Campbell
Typographer: E. Ann Yeoman

Canadian Cataloguing in Publication Data

Main entry under title:

Visions, ballet and its future

Proceedings of the National Ballet of Canada 25th
anniversary season dance conference held Nov. 15-16, 1976
at the Town Hall, St. Lawrence Centre for the Arts, Toronto.

Bibliography: p.
Includes index.
ISBN 0-88924-079-5 pa.

1. Ballet - Congresses. 2. Ballet - Canada -
Congresses. I. Crabb, Michael, 1947-
II. National Ballet of Canada.

GV1787.6.V58   792.8   C79-094152-X

PRINTED IN CANADA

We would like to express our appreciation to the following:
Wintario and the Samuel and Saidye Bronfman Family Foundation for their financial support.
Betty Oliphant, Elaine Campbell, Vincent Tovell and Gerry Eldred for their conception and creation of The National Ballet of Canada's 25th Anniversary Conference.

Marian M. Wilson, Publisher

CONTENTS

FOREWORD

Sir Frederick Ashton

One of the disadvantages of getting old is the way people assume one is the repository of great wisdom and insight into all kinds of things. It does not seem to make any difference how often I tell people that I have no views about anything and that if I have a philosophy it is to be found in my ballets. They still expect answers.

It was from a conviction that I had nothing worth saying that I firmly resisted contributing to the National Ballet of Canada's 25th Anniversary Conference. There was really little I could add to what such luminaries as Dame Ninette de Valois or Robert Joffrey had to say.

However, I am delighted to welcome this collection of essays, derived from the conference. The fact that the conference was held at all, quite apart from the enthusiastic support it excited, shows how wonderfully developed the art of dance has become in the public mind. It is particularly encouraging to find so much interest among the young people, which only goes to confirm what I have always believed. If ballet is anything, it is a form of artistic expression that penetrates far more deeply than words. People still crave beauty and poetry in art and it is because of this deeply-rooted human need that ballet will continue to have a central place among the performing arts.

Of course, it has been fashionable from time to time to pronounce the imminent death of ballet. It amuses me, however, to see how quickly fashions pass. Art must grow from tradition and be founded in a craft. I am glad to see among the contributions in this book a reassertion of the need for basic craftsmanship. If ballet, like any other art, is going to communicate, it must possess a language that its audience can understand. There must be some structure and sense of purpose to what appears on the stage. It is not enough for the artist, whether he be a dancer, a choreographer, designer or musician, merely to display his own private creative impulse. It is not enough to simply string steps together.

You may begin to think that I am a hopeless reactionary. Certainly I am a traditionalist in my respect for the heritage of ballet. I am a believer in the link in the chain. Anyone who imagines that the future of art lies in a rejection of the past is unrealistic. Nevertheless, I may add that as a choreographer I prefer not to dwell on what I have already accomplished and would therefore encourage those who read these essays to absorb the wisdom contained in them but always to look forward.

I seem to have contradicted what I said earlier about having no views about anything. In fact, I have probably expressed rather too many views here. Still, there is one more I would like to add. If you are an artist, remember that you are communicating to an audience of some sort and there is one sin no audience will excuse or forgive—boredom.

INTRODUCTION
Vincent Tovell

Toward the end of two exhausting days a young student from the National Ballet School asked for the floor. "I would just like to say that this conference has really gotten my head going," she began. "I have an incredible headache, but it's a very good one and I don't know if I'll be able to sleep for the next three weeks. I just really got inspired. I hope I can contribute somehow." She was promptly cheered and the verdict was in. Success!

The conference was to be "a celebration and exploration," a celebration of the National Ballet of Canada's 25th anniversary and an exploration of ballet's future here and around the world. It grew to be an international gala of artists, critics and administrators, and an open house for an audience of some 300 dancers, dance students, teachers, trustees, journalists and friends, in the midst of the company's splendid fall anniversary season. The Canadian Broadcasting Corporation summed it up a few days later for a national radio audience, and now this volume records the most important aspects of what was said. It may be an unprecedented distillation of several lifetimes of brilliant artistic achievement.

It is difficult to capture in print the spirit of the event. The fun, the enthusiasm, the sense of occasion, and the unexpectedly touching moments, were pure theatre. With such performers, how could it be otherwise? Still, the record is welcome. It includes wise and sensible warnings, and it documents a memorable and important event. The reader may imagine for himself the alert and eager students, the laughter and the lively discussions in the intervals, as four generations of enthusiasts mingled in the lobbies of the St. Lawrence Centre in Toronto.

It was Timothy Porteous, Associate Director of the Canada Council, who pointed out that when the legislation establishing the Council was drawn up in 1957, no mention was made of dance at all. It was a minor concern at that time. Today, dance finances (and politics) preoccupy the Canada Council, and provincial arts councils too, with money still lamentably scarce in proportion to need. Demands of many sorts press in from all sides and new companies keep appearing. Matters of priorities, standards, and disbursement of public subsidies have become extraordinarily complex in all the arts. They bedevil councils, as well as the voluntary boards who guide most arts organizations and, of course, they trouble dancers along with the rest, since sometimes they too get caught up in the passionate politics of poverty that threaten to pitch them each against all.

Most people would say that it is public funding that has brought dance and dancers to a new prominence in Canada—that, and a growing international awareness and appreciation of the art. Obviously, the new money has established a more solid professional base, but some important companies were in existence before the Canada Council was created.

In fact, the history of ballet in Canada stretches back to the early years of the century, when famous foreign artists and companies visited the main centres and Canadians, such as Boris Volkoff, taught and mounted special productions. The National Ballet of Canada was itself officially founded in 1951.

In 1938, two English women, Gweneth Lloyd and Betty Farrally, started their Winnipeg Ballet Club, which was eventually incorporated as a professional company in February, 1949. By 1953 it had become the Royal Winnipeg Ballet and has since made extensive tours around the world.

The Winnipegers were at the centre of an annual series of Canadian Ballet Festivals, from 1948 to 1954, which helped to focus the activities of teachers, dancers and budding choreographers from across the country.

In fact, Celia Franca saw the performances at the 1950 festival in Montreal. On the advice of Ninette de Valois, whose company, the Sadler's Wells Ballet, had made a triumphant visit to Toronto in 1949, Celia Franca had been invited by a group of Toronto ballet-lovers to establish a national company for Canada.

Leaving behind her promising career in England as a noted demi-caractère and choreographer, she dedicated herself for the next 24 years to building a classical repertory ballet company in Canada. There were many years of hard struggle, financial crises and exhausting tours, but the National Ballet of Canada steadily gained in quality and reputation. An ambitious repertoire was developed and associations were formed with such distinguished figures as Erik Bruhn, who staged and danced in his own productions of *Swan Lake* (1967) and *Coppélia* (1975), and Rudolf Nureyev, who starred in his lavish version of *The Sleeping*

Beauty (1972). In due course, international attention came with success in New York, Britain and Europe.

In 1959, a residential ballet school had been founded in Toronto with Betty Oliphant at its head, and from the school a succession of excellent dancers has moved into the company and the profession at large, assuring a continuity of technique and style that is now evident. Today, the separately constituted National Ballet School, still with Miss Oliphant as its director and principal, is considered among the best of its kind in the world.

At about the time the Royal Winnipeg and the National Ballet companies were being founded, Ludmilla Chiriaeff was establishing Les Grands Ballets Canadiens in Montreal, with dancers who had appeared for her on CBC television since the early fifties. Known at first mainly in Quebec, the youngest of the three "majors" in Canada has now also toured internationally with a broad repertoire of classical and contemporary ballets, several of them choreographed by Brian Macdonald.

Together, these three are the most prominent elements in a dance culture which today includes several small chamber groups and a variety of modern and experimental companies. A recent festival of contemporary dance, held in Toronto for three weeks, displayed more than 20 companies from across the country.

The scale and range of development in this quarter-century could not have been imagined a generation ago. Hundreds of artists are now earning a living, of sorts, in the dance professions and new audiences are still being discovered.

It is certain that none of this could have happened without federal and provincial grants, but it has been a collective achievement. Devoted artists, administrators, volunteers, trustees and funders together have transformed the scene. The artists in particular subsidized the growth with exhausting sacrifices. Performances in the main cities and small towns, on long and difficult tours, as well as on CBC television, have made them known and welcome. If their place in the public mind is now secure, it is their own doing. Great traditions appear to have taken root and as Charles Lussier, Director of the Canada Council, said in a gracious introduction to the conference, "the future is in good hands."

The conference recorded here had itself the form of a ballet in six acts, with plenty of occasions for spontaneous variations.

The overture: Dame Ninette de Valois, to set themes (the need for traditions, "national" styles, repertoire, and the care and nurture of dancers) with comments from Arnold Spohr, Artistic Director of the Royal Winnipeg Ballet; Ludmilla Chiriaeff, Founder and Director of Les Grands Ballets Canadiens; Alexander Grant, appointed successor to David Haber in 1976 as Artistic Director of the National Ballet; Veronica Tennant, prima ballerina of the company; and Margaret Dale, formerly a soloist of the Sadler's Wells Ballet in London, BBC-TV producer, and teacher at York University in Toronto. The points of reference for what was to follow were soon clear: the need for traditions from which significant innovation can grow, and the threats to those very traditions.

Then, head on and with eyes open—the matter of money. Timothy Porteous of the Canada Council had no particularly good news, no easy solutions. What funders do these days? But Peter Brinson, formerly director of "Ballet For All" and now with the Gulbenkian Foundation in London, made practical and provocative suggestions. His plea for long-range policies, and his stress on the responsibilities of private financiers and educational institutions—reprinted here in full—should be given careful attention and wide dissemination. It is perhaps inevitable that the funding section of this book should be the longest.

The critics too had their hour, with Clive Barnes, now of the *New York Post,* John Percival of the *Times* in London, and William Littler of the *Toronto Star*, convincingly arguing a modest role for the journalist, the newspaper reviewer, and drawing attention to the greater sophistication of audiences everywhere. This in turn will require of critics a wider and deeper knowledge of traditions and techniques.

The Canadian composers, Louis Applebaum and Harry Freedman, the American composer, Lukas Foss, and George Crum, the National Ballet's musical director (since the earliest days) each touched on the fundamentals of the relationship between music and dance, composers and choreographers—the sorts of collaboration essential for theatre magic. And, as they were joined for an extraordinary orchestration of talent by the American designer, Ming Cho Lee, the choreographer Brian Macdonald, then Artistic Director of Les Grands Ballets Canadiens, Robert Joffrey, Rudi van Dantzig of the Dutch

National Ballet and Dame Ninette de Valois, the discussion soon modulated, not surprisingly, into a spontaneous homage to Diaghilev, the Russian-born impresario who, in the early years of this century, returned ballet to the West and revolutionized every aspect of it. The dreams of a fusion—or fission—of stars, a big theatre bang, are as attractive now as ever. All that's wanted is a new Diaghilev and pots of money.

Fantasies aside, there was some sage and practical talk about urgent matters: Dame Ninette's call for "well-informed scenarios" that people will pay money to see again and again, and Louis Applebaum's concern for new and different uses of dance on television, and Ming Cho Lee's cry for a better training of theatre designers. The panelists may or may not have foretold the future but they faced the present squarely.

In her overture, Dame Ninette had in fact looked ahead, and warned that a too sudden and helter-skelter muddling of traditions—the trend today in the jet age—would exact an artistic price. We risk a loss of direction and continuity. The challenge to the young will be to learn what to hold on to and what to add. Others on the panels, just as strongly, argued the advantages of mixing people up, combining styles and techniques. It is not that they were in total disagreement, but the universe of dance is expanding in bewildering ways and the public appetite seems to grow by what it feeds on. Too much *can* happen too soon.

One may wonder what caused this explosion—this "dance swell" as Ludmilla Chiriaeff called it—at this particular time. Perhaps it is that, in Arnold Spohr's words, "dance is the easiest, strongest communication force in the world," transcending speech, frontiers, prejudices and generations, speaking to the imagination and to the heart. It is an international language we now know we need. The young in particular seem to feel this. The oldest of the arts, "the most basic and elemental of all our impulses delineated in the most sublime of human terms,"—as Charles Lussier called it—is at this time the newest.

Canada is a dance centre now and distinctive Canadian approaches are developing. How appropriate that on this occasion, the majority of the conference audience were students.

PREFACE

The task of editing the proceedings of the National Ballet of Canada's 25th Anniversary Conference has been made much easier by the generosity of the Canadian Broadcasting Corporation, who recorded everything that was said, and of the National Ballet itself, who assumed the unenviable task of producing a transcript from the tapes.

Generally, the major addresses by keynote speakers have been printed in their entirety with only occasional and minor stylistic changes. There is an exception to this rule.

The conference sessions dealing with the ballet in its relation to film, television and video, took the form of screenings with a minimum of talk around them. However, the subject of dance and the screen media recurred throughout the conference. It seemed important and appropriate to include the subject in this printed record. Thus, two leading authorities, Norman Campbell and Margaret Dale, both of whom participated in the conference, accepted invitations to write special essays for this collection. Their comments reflect and summarize opinions and concerns expressed at various points during the conference.

An important part of the conference was occupied by the

comments of those invited to sit on panels for each session and by the general discussion that resulted during the question periods. Editing this material presented some difficult problems. Sometimes discussion veered well off topic and, while interesting when heard during the actual conference, seemed unsuitable for inclusion here. There was also a problem of space, since to publish everything would have required a very large book indeed.

We have tried to condense and summarize the most important points brought out in discussion, wherever possible making them flow naturally from the themes and ideas presented in the major papers. As a result, the amount of recorded commentary is uneven from section to section. Not all subjects generated the same amount of talk.

Each unit in this book stands well on its own and therefore we felt confident in rearranging the order of presentation from that of the conference. The order we have chosen seems to us more suitable for the printed page where, it is hoped, readers will want to pause and consider what they have read. We believe there is a more logical flow to this arrangement.

Naturally, we share with the National Ballet of Canada and the publishers our appreciation for all those whose financial support has made the appearance of this volume possible.

Michael Crabb
Editor
Holly Small
Assistant Editor

VISIONS

BALLET
and DANCERS

Dame Ninette de Valois

Alexander Grant   Veronica Tennant   Arnold Spohr
Ludmilla Chiriaeff   Margaret Dale

What do we mean by "style" in ballet? How important is tradition? Does a ballet need a story? Should the ballet and modern dance feed on and learn from each other, or should they remain discrete?

These were only some of the questions, "red herrings" as she called them, in Dame Ninette de Valois' opening address to the conference, with which she hoped to "get the ball rolling." In fact, as the ensuing papers and commentary in this book reveal, Dame Ninette's remarks had more the effect of a bombshell—though a benign one. Right at the start of the conference it was demonstrated that ballet is a vital, controversial art able to stir the passions of its devotees in many different and not always complementary ways. Complacency is the death of any art. Ninette de Valois makes sure none of us remains complacent.

BALLET and DANCERS

Dame Ninette de Valois
Red Herrings

May I start by saying what a very great honour it is for me to be with you here, and please realize the real appreciation and admiration I have had from the National Ballet of Canada's performances in the last few days. It is a great achievement in 25 years. I have not only attended the performances, but have seen the work going on in the National Ballet School, so I want to offer my congratulations of course to Celia Franca for her marvellous job in building the Company and I also want to add to her name Miss Betty Oliphant, who has done all the work in the School.

Having said that, it seems to be my job to lay down a few "red herrings" that you can pick up and discuss. My idea is really to get the ball rolling for this Conference.

I would like to start with the important question

of style in ballet. The word "style" is used so often (and frivolously) today in relation to ballet, but without much thought to its meaning.

As I see it, style in ballet can be analyzed in varying ways. First, I see what I call school style. This is a traditional evolution from a classical pedagogy developed over the centuries. The next is what I'm going to call psychological style, and it includes temperament that is racial in its implications and includes very clearly defined physical types to be found in various parts of the world in various dancers' bodies. Then again there is a choreographic style, the result of creativity from the two sources already mentioned—school and native inheritance.

Here we reach a point that must be watched with great care. The speed of everything today, the terrible speed of getting everywhere and doing everything in five minutes, has produced a rapid growth of ballet. Today ballets and ballet companies can be launched so quickly—dancers collected from everywhere and great tours embarked upon. It's very different from the picture of 25 years ago in Canada and 50 years ago in England. The enormous inheritance of choreographic works can be picked up anywhere. The danger is, will this affect individual national ballet styles? One cannot be so narrow-minded as not to see the importance of internationalism, but please, let us look at ourselves, particularly when we are national ballets, as having our own individual style. Of course, this brings us to the great source, to the great schools: the Italian, the French, the Danish and the Russian. Everything that has emerged in the last 50 years or so has sprung from chosen roots and bits and pieces from each other. But all of them, if you watch them, also have their individual school style that comes out in their dancers and in their choreographers. We must be very careful, with all the "national" ballets that have been so admirably and speedily coming to the front today. They have to grow and develop just as their predecessors. Borrow what you like, but from your borrowings, develop yourselves. This is what I'm a little bit frightened may get lost in the present frenzy of company building. Tradition is not to be sneered at; it is terribly important. We must face that every country has its individual approach to everything, whether it is a dance, painting or drama, and we can't afford to lose that. It must creep into the ballet world just as well as it does into all the other arts. We must have a firm national strain in our work and we must develop and national style of our dances.

One can observe how others, having absorbed the traditional pedagogy, found a source of their own style in their national dances. The whole of Western Europe is renowned for its speed, its precision, its lightness, its impeccable exactitude in everything it does. We spring mainly from the French, Italian and Danish schools. But we all spring from the same tradition of relaxed social dancing. When I say "social dancing," I don't mean ballroom dancing. I go right back to native dances, the natural expression through hundreds of years of the man in the street expressing himself through what he feels is his natural movement.

With us in Western Europe, it is very much from the waist down. We have this extraordinary attack. Look at the clog dances, look at the basque dances with their *entrechats*, introduced to the Paris Opera when it was developing its classical school. Look at these things and remember that this is a part of our native style we must not lose.

Now the Russian ballet, when it started, absorbed western pedagogy naturally into itself and, in doing so, slowly evolved its own style. What do you see behind it? You see the wonderful quality of their approach to national dances expressed right through the whole body with certain, even Eastern, influences in the hand movements and the body movements. It's different, as different as it could possibly be and it's so right that it has now permeated the Russian classical school and given it this really marvellous plastic quality. Now, this plastic quality is theirs, just as the speed and precision of our school is ours, and I would suggest to you that we look at it with care. In each case, we can help one another by ironing out weaknesses and strengthening certain things in our own schools.

We have influenced the Russians in their footwork and they are beginning to influence us in our movement generally. But still we must turn to our choreographers, we must turn to our own traditions, to give our companies their own style. When I say style, I don't mean characterization. Oddly enough, the characterization of any type of dance from any country is highlighted if there is a definite style. If there isn't a definite style present, the characterization will not be accurate.

I want to move on to another important matter, the position of music today in the ballet world. Perhaps I'm just too old to be "with it," but I feel we are losing our contact with composers. This is very wrong. It is time that the ballet world turn to its different composers in each country and really work from such a basic inspiration.

One has only to go back through the Russian repertory, or for that matter the French or Danish, to see that the ballets that have best endured were worked from scratch with the choreographer and composer following a mutually agreeable structure. I mention the word structure since it is woefully missing in so much of today's ballet. I mean by it a well-formed scenario. It is a problem that must be attended to. We were very disciplined in this regard years ago and look what a heritage of ballets were left and that still live and live.

What happens today is that somebody gets an idea and looks for a piece of music, or they hear a piece of music and think, "I could do some movements to that." Away they go and, half the time, there is no image in it. I don't like this approach to choreography. Of course, there are instances such as Fokine's *Les Sylphides* where existing music and movement have been combined wonderfully, but the prevailing trend was otherwise and it's something we will have to come back to. We must get the composers interested in ballet again. When we started the Sadler's Wells Ballet in the thirties, I had at least eight distinguished British composers at work on new ballets for us!

Of course, there is a terrible snobbery about the distinction between writing for a ballet and writing for an opera. For some extraordinary reason, most composers would rather write an opera, which may only be put on once every ten years to a half-full house, than a ballet that can go on forever, year after year. But then, I think we're not interesting enough for the musicians at the moment and we have got to do something about this.

I'm giving you a great deal to argue about and there is a third little point I would like to mention and that is the question of classical and contemporary dance. I feel one thing very strongly and it is a compliment to both sides. I wish they would stay severely apart, do the work they are meant to do and not get too involved with each other. You cannot be fully trained as a classical dancer with all that it demands of you and serve the contemporary dance anything like the way a fully trained contemporary dancer can. I saw the Martha Graham season at Covent Garden and know the delights the contemporary dance can rise to. I loved every moment of it, but I didn't want to see any classical dancer come on and try to do what those admirable Graham dancers were doing with such perfection.

Every genre of dance that has its roots in the theatre has something to offer the others. There are many beautiful movements and exercises from the contemporary dance that we may appreciate and use. And I believe it is very common for certain classical exercises now to be accepted in the contemporary dance world. There is a similar fusion of ballet with character work. But there is no school as strict as a pure classical school, and we have to keep this alive, particularly in our national dance theatres. Audiences have reached such a pitch of aesthetic appreciation that, in their demand for pure classicism they are intolerant of what they know to be impure.

We move from that to the gymnasts and here I am a little more severe. Please leave them to their own game. We would not have so many accidents in the ballet world if we knew where the gymnasts stopped and the dancers started. As a trained classical dancer and teacher, I don't like to see lovely little girl gymnasts doing a sort of dance in the middle of the arena, at which, if she were a dancer, you would exclaim, "Oh, how awful, that child has been hopelessly overstrained! What is going to happen to her in a few years?" While we may examine technically and very carefully what can be learned from the gymnasts, our two worlds are separate and must remain so.

I have scattered quite a few red herrings before you, so pick them up and have some fun!

Dame Ninette de Valois' provocative address did exactly what she intended it to do. It set a tone of inquiry for the whole conference, one bridging the past and the future. It stimulated debate and introduced issues that kept bubbling to the surface in many of the sessions to follow.

Alexander Grant, Artistic Director of the National Ballet of Canada, was quick to take up Dame Ninette's point about acrobatics and ballet:

"I have listened very carefully, as always, to what Dame Ninette has said and I must smile a little bit....I have appeared in two ballets she choreographed. In *Job* I had to roll downstairs, a series of stairs in fact, ending up with my head flat on the floor. *The Rake's Progress*, perhaps her most famous ballet, finished with me falling over and balancing on my head!" Dame Ninette defended herself briskly by declaring it had been Robert Helpmann who had, against her wishes, introduced that particular trick to *The Rake's Progress*, after which his successors in the role insisted on repeating it. "Every choreographer suffers from the dancer who comes along and inserts something the choreographer did not want done. I told Robert Helpmann and the others that they would finish up with bad necks!" That still left *Job* unexplained, to which Grant added the case of Dame Ninette's *Don Quixote* in which she had him crawl around on his hands and knees as Sancho Panza—with Robert Helpmann on his back.

A number of Dame Ninette's other points were taken up and developed by her fellow panelists during their ensuing commentary and in the question period.

Arnold Spohr, for more than 20 years Artistic Director of the Royal Winnipeg Ballet, had fewer misgivings about the growing internationalism of the ballet. "We all feed one another, learning from one another, belonging to one another. The dance language is the easiest, strongest communicative force in the world. There is a special bond among dancers, a general vibrant glow."

This universality of the language of ballet, in Alexander Grant's view, made a growing internationalism inevitable. Even if economic factors restrict the international movement of whole companies, individual dancers and choreographers will move beyond the companies that have fostered them. "An artist nowadays can reach even my home country, New Zealand, in a matter of two days from any part of the world. A definite advantage, I might add, for New Zealand. Again, the magic of dance notation systems means a ballet can be put in an envelope and posted across the world.

"All this does not help those who want a company to be a tight little island, and there is a great deal to be said for tight little islands if they are a hotbed of creativity....But, like it or not, the future will see a greater coming and going of both performing and creative artists. The danger in all this is that many companies will be presenting the same repertoire and artists. Let us not be too disconcerted by this, as so do the best opera houses, dramatic theatres and, for that matter, concert halls.

"Perhaps this is the price of ballet's development and recognition as a worldwide art....The challenge is there, the field is larger, and the future of ballet very healthy."

Grant's fundamental optimism was generally shared although some of his colleagues had important reservations or concerns. Ludmilla Chiriaeff, founder and director of Les Grands Ballets Canadiens, aptly summed up the extraordinary growth of ballet by coining a phrase, which has since been widely repeated, when she referred to the "dance swell." Veronica Tennant, the National Ballet's senior ballerina, provided statistics for the phenomenal growth of her own company's audience and Arnold Spohr drew attention to the significant growth of dance in the universities and to the popularizing influence of today's ballet superstars, Nureyev and Baryshnikov.

For those such as Spohr and Chiriaeff whose memories extend to the early, bleak days of Canadian ballet, the contrast was poignant and for them a vindication of what they had always believed to be the fundamental and lasting importance of dance as a human activity. "The road travelled is long," said Madame Chiriaeff. "What I find the greatest achievement is that dance, which was once the exclusive property of the elite, has widely overflown this limited setting." "In no age can man live by his intellect alone," stated Spohr. "The emotional life must find some outlet. The exhilaration of vigorous rhythmic movement can be found directly in social dancing and in the theatre by vicarious participation. Dance will continue as long as the rhythmic flow of energy operates and until man ceases to respond to the forces of life and the universe."

Ludmilla Chiriaeff extended her remarks to touch upon another of Dame Ninette de Valois' topics, that of national style. The nature of dance as an art form, "a declaration of the human being's needs, desires, even hallucinations in a given place and point of time, creates a two-way link with the cultures of people. It is this double adherence that gives art, and naturally dance, its deepest significance as a means of expression and communication."

The dance artists must draw not only upon learned pedagogical traditions but also on the traditions of their origins to identify themselves with their own culture. "Only then will their product be truly valid and significant." As Veronica Tennant put it, "Through the expression of dance one can still speak of mystery, magic and love. We are at liberty to escape from our world or comment on it. In our medium there are no limits imposed on one of man's most precious yet waning gifts—imagination."

Margaret Dale returned the discussion to a more practical

note. A former dancer, television producer and, in 1976, head of the Dance Department at York University, she was concerned with the education of dancers beyond technique and performance. She feels there is need for a definite career structure that might lead the dancer into related professions either as an alternative to the stage or a succeeding occupation.

Dame Ninette suggested that the process of career structuring could occur naturally with a company and its school. "Very early along it is quite easy to recognize a budding *répétiteur*, teacher or notator. Ballet is a wide and varied field but it is up to the company staff and directors to encourage artists during their performing careers in directions we know they could succeed in later on."

The question of the "mature" (sometimes synonymous with "older") dancers arose. It was agreed that they had an important role to play in ensuring the passage of tradition from generation to generation and in defining style within their particular companies.

Dame Ninette de Valois' opening comments about style in ballet attracted further attention during the question period when she elaborated her earlier points. Pursuing her idea of the development of national styles in ballet, Dame Ninette considered it a slow process taking at least 25 years and closely associated with the continuous activity of choreographers.

"Frankly, you have to have your own choreographers who know what is coming out of your own roots. The native choreographers are the people who will discover what are your styles....You must turn to your own creativity while strengthening it with everything from the outside."

Ludmilla Chiriaeff's attitude was even more specific. "I believe very deeply that any art is only true when consciously or unconsciously it springs from the soil. Art is really a mirror to our identity. It is only by being ourselves that we can reach the international, because the strength of our message comes from the truth of being ourselves."

MUSIC and DANCE

Lukas Foss

George Crum   Harry Freedman   Louis Applebaum

Among her "red herrings" Ninette de Valois raised the question of music: "We must get the composers interested in ballet again." In the following section, four distinguished musicians present some of the problems and possibilities, both theoretical and practical, that insinuate themselves into the relationship of music and dance.

Lukas Foss investigates the ways in which that relationship has been conducted and asks if music and ballet can achieve an aesthetic unity.

George Crum examines more material, "logistical," problems. Harry Freedman looks for a return to the creative ferment of the Diaghilev era which, as Louis Applebaum suggests, may perhaps be rediscovered among the smaller dance troupes.

MUSIC and DANCE

Lukas Foss
The User and The Used

Dance and music have a common denominator: rhythm. In primitive cultures the word "dance" itself included the rhythm of drums, hand-clapping or foot-stamping, and all folk or pop dancing to this day implies a beat. In other words, movement with sound, dance with music.

As dance originally included the presence of music, so the ancient Greek word "music" assumed the presence of words. In every folksong we have "the perfect wedding of words and music," in every folk dance the perfect wedding of music and dance.

But if we open that Pandora's Box called "art," we are in trouble. Art separates, specializes, artificializes, combines rather than unites, contrives in order to relate.

In ballet, dance and music are partners, two separate entities, never equal. Wagner claimed equality of the visual, the literary and the musical in his *Gesamt-kunstwerk*. His *oeuvre* is a perfect example to the contrary, a testimony to the inegalitarian nature of artistic materials. One element dominates, the other supports. One uses, the other is used. In the tradition of ballet, the dance *uses* the music. The choreography helps itself to the composition. I have nothing against this relationship. To use is not necessarily to abuse.

I, for one, like to see my music used, and I am proud that a dozen scores of mine have been choreographed by some twenty dance companies. I wish composers would recapture some of the excitement of being involved with dance. My advice to them is: enjoy being used. There are even advantages: you are less dependent. The used does not need the user. The user always seeks, woos and cajoles the used. As the leader is lost without the led, so the user is lost without his object. Thus the music, in its subservient role, may dominate the scene, as The Maid dominates The Mistress in Genet's play. I am not, of course, speaking of strong music and weak dance; that would spell failure, which does not concern me here. I am speaking of the successful collaboration between good music and good dance.

Surely, there must be some objection: someone will say "Wait—can this not be reversed? Isn't the composer the user whenever the choreography precedes the music, when the composer watches the dance (performed for him in silence), notates the timing, the beats, the accents, then proceeds to compose the music?" I myself started out with such an experience as a teenage composer working for Doris Humphrey and Charles Weidman. I remember thinking then that what I was doing was an unnatural thing, that the normal procedure was being reversed for technical convenience, that Weidman would have ended up with a stronger work had he helped himself to the music prior to creating movement. Actually, for our thesis it is irrelevant which comes first, choreography or composition; in either instance it is still the choreographer who helps himself to the music.

I should like again to illuminate the relationship of dance to music by comparing it with the relationship of composition to poetry. Would a poet invent his poem to fit the notes? I have never heard of a good poem coming into existence in that manner. On the other hand, a lyricist will agree to fit his words and rhymes to a pop tune. It is a little awkward, but it is done. Great work, however, is not accomplished that way; the word filled with emotion bursts into song. A tune does not burst into words. Similarly, music may burst into dance, but the dance can at best have music fitted to it. The dancer-choreographer goes in search of his music. The composer does not go in search of his dance movement; if he does, he is the exception that proves the rule. I am belabouring the point to break through the persistent myth of music and dance being two interchangeable quantities.

Now, what are the prerequisites for the right use, for the right to use? Balanchine would say love, "love for the music." But to love does not necessarily give one the right to use, and certainly we don't have the right to use what we don't love. If a choreographer loves and uses bad music he might be guilty of bad taste. If he uses music without loving it, he will fail to

establish an interesting relationship. If he does not
love any music, he might as well use silence. Dance in
silence is effectively disembodied, although we do
miss the challenge, the relationship, the *im*perfect
marriage.

In one respect the choreographer-composer
relationship is comparable to the performer-composer
relationship, or the actor-drama relationship. Musical
performers as well as actors are like lovers who gain
their identity, their power, precisely by immersing
themselves in the object of that love. It is something
of a paradox that by "becoming" King Lear, or by
playing a Bach fugue you can "find yourself." But
that is the mystery inherent in the love relationship.
Thus, the choreographer will find himself by
immersion in the music he uses, the dancer in turn
will find himself by immersion in the ballet, in the
dance. This is often called "interpretation," which is
a misnomer. A lover does not interpret the loved one.
A dancer chooses the music the way one chooses a
mate. The same applies to the composer who sets a
poem to music. And incidentally, the poem does not
need him either, just as a Stravinsky or Tchaikowsky
score does not need the choreographer. In fact, even
if the composer enjoys the use of his score, the score
has a way of wanting to command the listener's entire
attention. Similarly, the poem wants to command the
reader's entire attention. Few poets desire to be set to
music. Quite a few forbid it. Every time I set a poem
I feel like shouting to the poet: "Rejoice! See how
well your poem is being used." More soberly I might
say "Forgive me....I am using you because I love you,
hence my music is a homage to your poem."

Every Balanchine ballet is an implied homage, an

implied dedication to the music it uses. I think there is something tragic about the choreographer's loving attempt to translate music in terms of dance movement, because translating one art into another is an art in itself, one that has not been invented and does not, in fact, exist.

Now, what does the dancer actually do when he choreographs a piece of music? What does he do with the music?

It seems to me he has three options: imitation, opposition and independence. The first, imitation, is a kind of cavalier-like transposition of aural movement to visual movement, a way of following the music. Its dangers are redundancy, duplication, pseudo-translation; a dubious approach to which we owe *all* our great ballets! The second, opposition, is the reverse of imitation, a contrived device used mostly for relief from the first option. For example, the music sustains a sound while the dancers use that very moment for maximum stage activity, or the music is all over the place while the dancers are motionless. In other words, it is a type of pseudo-counterpoint. Real counterpoint, just like real translation, demands equal elements. The third option, independence, allows the dance to ignore the music. This is the basis of the Cage/Cunningham collaboration. I quote Cage: "There is an independence of the music and dance. This independence follows from our faith that the support of the dance is not to be found in the music but in the dancer himself, on his own two legs, that is, and occasionally on a single one." Likewise, the music sometimes consists of single sounds or groups of sounds which are not separated by harmonies but resound within a space of silence. From this independence of music and dance, a rhythm results which is not that of horses' hoofs or other regular beats, but which reminds us of a multiplicity of events in time and space—stars in the sky, for instance, or activities on earth viewed from the air are *separate* activities. They ignore each other. There is no love relationship between choreography and music if they ignore each other, not even an imperfect wedding. There is no user and used, but, there is indeed equal partnership. How true to life! Equal partnership is obtained if you ignore each other, if relationship is avoided. What we get in this approach is sound in motion *plus* visual motion, what Joel Chadabe calls the additive principle as opposed to the interacting principle. We get music *plus* dance, not music interacting with dance. Erick Hawkins says, and I quote: "Movement and music put together without a common pulse is like two people talking to you at the same time." Cage would answer (and I am not quoting), "Why not? I like to hear the sound of people talking at the same time."

What is the way out of this labyrinth? Can't we achieve the simple, uncontrived, true unity of music and dance that we find in every primitive or ethnic dance? Alas, folk art is young art. It ages. No Beethoven sonata was ever as young as a rock song in the early days of rock, as a waltz when Strauss first presented it and the young made it into a way of life. And nothing is now more nostalgic, wistful, touchingly old, than the Viennese Waltz. As for the Beatles, their music will soon be grandfather's. But the Beethoven work was never young. It never had the scent of fresh flowers and it never faded. It is carved in rock. It is contrived. Art contrives. Art-music is contrived music. Art-dance is contrived dance. Contriving is a peculiarly human achievement. Only man contrives; he stylizes, he freezes things so they will last. He builds monuments that will outlive him.

We have seen that music and dance are "one" in primitive or folk expression only. In "art" there is a complex, even impossible love relationship between user and used, based on three unsatisfactory and contrived procedures: imitation, opposition, independence. This unsolvable and faulty state of affairs, however, is precisely what creates a challenging situation. ("My method does not quite work—that's why it's interesting." Arnold Schoenberg.) Art thrives on problematic situations demanding a maximum of contrivance and artifice. If I may quote a medieval philosopher: "God cannot be praised artificially enough."

The essentially unanswered paradox at the heart of Lukas Foss' profound and thoughtful paper was left to work on the minds of its listeners. Other panelists added to the amplitude of the discussion on music and dance by expressing concerns of particular importance to them.

George Crum

Some Logistical Snags

By virtue of a rather long association with a local dance troupe, I have been in a position to view first-hand the difficulties involved in providing the public with a balanced repertoire. To deal very briefly with the classical portion of that repertoire, I, along with many who know somewhat more about ballet, believe firmly that the great master works of the past must be performed on a regular basis, partly as a joy and partly as a discipline. That said, I should like to focus on the problems encountered by a major dance company in producing new works.

First, it can safely be said that today's ballet dancers are well equipped technically and temperamentally to cope with contemporary music. Stravinsky recalled in his autobiography that at the first performance of *The Rite of Spring,* far from sitting comfortably in his box, his services were required in the wings where he was obliged to shout out the counts for the suffering dancers. Today, dancers have a greater understanding of and appreciation for the music they perform. The problems don't lie with the dancers but rather with thorny things like finances, logistics and even personal attitudes.

For example, a composer sitting down to fulfil a commission for a symphonic score has a right to feel that his work will succeed according to the degree of his inspiration. A ballet score, on the other hand, requires a collective inspiration; many things must happen. First, someone must have an idea, a scenario perhaps, possibly a plot or even a purely expressive idea, but it must be a good one. Second, the composer must enter into collaboration with the choreographer and the choreographer must be a good one. This second point of early collaboration is often neglected. I receive a good many scores for perusal, always with a note attached assuring me that the enclosed tone poem would make an excellent ballet owing to what the senders call the "dance quality" of their music. Alternatively, they offer an hour-long score for which they themselves have worked out an elaborate scenario, usually dealing with some such subject as the winning of the West or conceivably the *War of the Worlds*, for which they assure me it would be possible to rent a real honest-to-God space ship from the Smithsonian Institute.

Incidentally, the collaboration I've been talking about can work both ways. Often the choreographer will seek out a composer. The important thing is that the composer and choreographer be in some kind of harmony. There are many other elements in the creation of a ballet: sets and costume designs, not to mention expert production and lighting crews. If any of these elements fail, everyone is in trouble. A fine score can be wrecked on the shoals of a mediocre scenario and a dull score will present an impossible obstacle to a talented choreographer.

Thus it is not surprising that a ballet company might approach a commissioned ballet with some degree of apprehension, since a failure of any element in the structure is likely to result in a large budgetary fiasco, requiring a most understanding board of directors.

I am a musician and have no talent for and certainly no heart for financial affairs. But I must mention what I consider to be the very discouraging fees expected by many publishers today for performing rights. A full evening ballet by a famous composer cost our company, in 1972, $150 per performance for the grand rights. In contrast, only four years later, when we negotiated for a much shorter work, not in fact an original composition but a rearrangement of a 19th century score, the publisher's first demand was for over $2000 per performance, plus a percentage of the gross. This figure was later renegotiated and now remains at a flat $1320 a performance. So despite our desire to keep the work in the permanent repertoire, a fee as high as this might prove an irresistible deterrent.

One last practical matter. Please, Mr. Composer, keep in mind that a ballet company, especially on tour, does not normally count among its orchestral resources a quartet of contrabass clarinets, six heavy-duty vacuum cleaners tuned in augmented fourths and one 2000 horsepower Pratt and Whitney aircraft engine! Stay, dear composer, within the fairly reasonable instrumental conventions and we ballet companies will perform with pleasure all the beautiful ballet scores you can dream up and we can pay for.

George Crum's explanation came as a shock to many audience members who had never realized the enormous costs of musical presentation. That, however, did not dissuade the next panelist, Canadian composer Harry Freedman, from challenging the National Ballet's general failure to commission new scores, a point he underlined by reference to the exciting cultural ferment of the Diaghilev era. Even a major classical repertory company, founded on the principle of restaging traditional, time-honoured works, should also be braving new artistic frontiers.

What I want to say might be described as a theme with variations and it begins with the matter of choreographers creating ballets to existing music. George Crum has already ennumerated some of the things that deter choreographers from commissioning original scores. In addition to which, radio and phonographic records have made it so easy for choreographers to shop around.

Harry Freedman

The Ambience of Creativity

You have all seen ballets inspired by a choreographer's excited response to a piece of music that has attracted him. It can be marvellous. But the

overwhelming majority of ballets that have endured
were created to music written especially for them. It is
not a mere coincidence, either. There is something
special about dancers learning a piece of original
choreography, but imagine the increased excitement
when the music is also fresh and original. Such a
creative milieu produces a ferment that is much more
than the sum of its individual parts. It vitalizes the
whole performing company.

The Diaghilev company has of course become
famous for its intense, concentrated creative
productivity. A list of the names of his dancers,
choreographers, composers, painters, writers and
designers reads like a Who's Who of ballet. However,
all this is very wrongly tossed off by saying that it was
easy for Diaghilev to do what he did when he had
artists of the stature of Picasso and Stravinsky
working for him. The implication of course is that we
do not have any contemporary Picassos or
Stravinskys. Perhaps not, but just remember that
Diaghilev, while he did discover a few unknown
geniuses, also used many well-established figures.
Also, we tend to forget the people he took up with
equal enthusiasm and expectations who did not turn
out to be winners. Hardly anyone could name them.

But just because they were not winners misses the
whole point about Diaghilev. First, remember he had
an incredible knack of getting, sometimes of dragging,
the very best from people. There are stories of Picasso
tearing up sketches in a rage rather than re-do them
according to Diaghilev's suggestions and now that
Stravinsky's note books have been published we can
see the many changes that took place in composing
The Rite of Spring, often at Diaghilev's suggestion.
Second, Diaghilev had an obsession with newness.

That's not always a virtue, but it was in his case. It was this aspect of Diaghilev's character that caused him to gather creative people around him. The hallmark of Diaghilev's career, as I read it, is the ambience of creativity he produced, that excited and inspired his company, and resulted in all those incredible works.

In Canada, from my observation, there are two companies that have followed the path set by Diaghilev. The National Ballet, I'm sorry to say, is not one of them. Veronica Tennant has told us she would like to be pushed, challenged and inspired. Good for her. She would like to perform in the classics of tomorrow. There is only one way that can be done. It can't be achieved just by having superb dancers as indeed the National Ballet does. You have to involve all the other people: composers, choreographers, writers, painters, designers. Those are the people who are going to create the ferment that will inspire and excite.

Composing is not a very visible activity. It takes place, if you are lucky, in a lonely, quiet room. The only sounds are the sounds in the composer's head and the only activity is the same composer writing down all those funny looking hieroglyphics on a piece of paper with a whole lot of lines ruled on it. Max Ferguson once introduced me on a radio program by saying, "He's a composer. He writes his own music. But of course, he uses that paper with the lines already printed, so all he has to do is fill in the notes." Dear Max!

Perhaps because composing is not a visible activity, it is a little known fact that 1976 also marks the 25th anniversary of the Canadian League of

Composers. Here we have two organizations that were created in the same year, grew up side by side, two organizations that represent inextricably entwined disciplines and yet, in the past 25 years, there has been really very little collaboration between the National Ballet and members of the League. I think it would be rather nice if during the next 25 years we got together. As Lukas Foss said, "We would love to be used."

Louis Applebaum took up a number of points raised earlier in the session. He saw great hope for creativity in the smaller dance troupes.

"These ventures grow out of a new thought, a new desire, a new ambition, and do not necessarily fall into the patterns established by our grand and marvellous big companies."

As a composer as well as an arts administrator, Mr. Applebaum could not sympathize with George Crum's concern for composer's royalties. Generally the creators, composers and choreographers, who live on fees rather than salaries, are the worst paid. It is just and inevitable that they should expect royalties.

The subject of money was a major element in the question period that followed. George Crum agreed that a living composer had a right to be paid but even in 1972 it had irked him to have to pay $150 per performance to the publishers of a composer who had been dead for 20 years.

There were complaints about the general quality of playing by ballet orchestras. George Crum was again ready with some practical explanations. Except in a few cases where companies are part of an opera house with a large, permanent orchestra, there is often difficulty in gathering together sufficient musicians for a big symphonic score such as Prokofiev's *Romeo and Juliet*. Even if the orchestra can be successfully contracted, a nerve-wracking business on tour, there is no guarantee they will fit into the pit or that the conductor will be able to see them all once they are there.

The design of many theatres, even those recently built, has paid scant attention to the needs of live musical performance. Symphony orchestras are not expected to give concerts from a hole in the ground. Ballet orchestras often are. In addition to which, the scheduling of orchestra rehearsal is a major problem.

Lukas Foss suggested that Stravinsky had pointed the way with *L'Histoire du soldat*, which did not need a hundred musicians to play it. Perhaps composers should take more account of the apparently insurmountable practical problems of live music for dance. Foss admitted that Stravinsky himself had sometimes forgotten the servant role of the composer in ballet, creating scores so overbearing that it was almost impossible for the visual elements to cope with writing of such scale and force.

The question of the relationship of the composer to the dance was never settled; not surprising, since there is no final answer. However, Harry Freedman described his own excitement in being part of a long-term project, the creation of a ballet, which might go on being modified even after its first performance. "When you have finished the score, that is only the beginning."

To an extent, the composer is bound to be forced into certain restrictions by the demands of a choreographer. Music heard at the same time as related movement is being danced will not necessarily be the same when played alone, which accounts for the common habit of composers to rearrange ballet scores if they are to be given in concert.

The session devoted to music in ballet highlighted the extreme complexity of the subject, offering ideas, sometimes solutions, that ranged from quasi-metaphysical speculation to hard, practical truths. From it, however, emerged a general feeling that ballet, and dance in general, must find ways to overcome any obstacles in order to produce the kind of creative ferment from which sprung the great ballets of the past.

DESIGN

Ming Cho Lee

After two sessions it had become clear that the ghost of Diaghilev could not be laid to rest. His achievement in presiding over an almost perfect union of music, movement and design was continually in the minds of conference members.

In the case of design, Ming Cho Lee, having defined the designer's function, expressed doubt about the adequacy of his training in North America. Even a bare stage makes a visual statement of sorts and the person making that statement must be an artist with a sensitivity to the peculiar needs of dance. "Craft" alone is not sufficient.

DESIGN

Ming Cho Lee

Making Visual Statements

Whenever I am invited to a conference to talk about design, I am always put in mind of the occasion some years ago when I happened to be giving a joint lecture at the University of Texas in Austin with that great designer, Donald Oenslager. Actually, I was conducting a seminar of graduate students when one tall young Texan just could not hold himself in any longer and very bluntly said: "What do you guys do?" Being fairly quick of mind, I replied: "It is less a matter of what we do; more a question of the *function* we perform." I explained that it does not really matter who does it, but that in the theatre, somebody has to make the visual decisions. It could be the janitor, but it has to be done. That is what we do.

We are collaborators in the total venture, ones specializing in making visual statements about something that is essentially non-visual, whether it be words, music or movement. We have an important share in the overall visual statement. Even if you come in and discover what you like to call a bare stage, that is still a visual statement. And, as a matter of fact, it is a very difficult one to make. Do you want to hide the hanging-lines and so on? If you do, then you have not got a bare stage. You are still confronted with a visual choice.

The designer for ballet and dance has a particularly tricky job to do. It is not quite the same with the lighting designer or the costume designer—and I realize sometimes costumes and set are done by the same person. The dance, with a few exceptions, needs light and costumes. It is more subtle with stage design. I say this because of my perception of the nature of dance as a theatrical art.

To my mind, dance, ballet, theatrical movement, call it what you will, is the purest and least literal form of theatre. It is akin to music in that sense. In fact, I have always felt that the more literal dance becomes the less it is truly dance. It may be mime—often very bad mime—but it loses the special purity dance should have as a medium of expression in the theatre.

Perhaps that is why I do not believe film or television (allowing for some remarkable successes) can handle dance. Film has a totally different kind of flexibility. It has no limits in space. It can go anywhere. It is multi-focal. You have long shots and close-ups. Those wonderful effects! Who can forget Vivien Leigh standing there in *Gone With the Wind*, saying, "I'll never hunger again," or whatever it was she did say? That's film, but it is not theatre.

In real theatre you are here, alive, seeing the space. It is limited. We are limited, sitting in a certain position. It creates a feeling of one being part of a family, locked in one space. And even though we may have a proscenium arch, if a member of the audience leaves, the performer will know. Maybe he is just tip-toeing out or is stalking out in anger. There is a reaction.

The eye has a lens with a fixed focal length. We cannot zoom in. We are perceiving space and volume in a very special way. It controls our whole perception of the spacing of movement and dancers. We are made highly conscious of how many bodies are there, what they are doing, what their relationship is to each other. When people forget these basic spatial visual considerations of the live theatre the result is usually disaster.

Because ballet and dance are such pure visual forms of theatre they can achieve a tremendous emotional impact in a clear space. You have seen this kind of ballet. Most of George Balanchine's ballets have been created with just a plain blue backdrop—in effect, empty space. Some call it the pure classical form. Dancers come and go, in and out, from the wings. There is beautiful lighting and perhaps costumes, often just leotards, but essentially it is through movement alone that theatre happens. Now, if you impose other visual elements onto that kind of work, one that is really complete in itself, your design is quite likely to be superfluous. It becomes merely decorative.

We designers want to be more than interior decorators. (I hope there are none listening. I will have made them very angry.) The lighting is different.

It becomes a moving force along with the dance itself, or it may simply be creating a clear space for the movement. The costume, of course, is part of the dancer's body.

Things are a little different when we turn to dance, in which the space needs defining more particularly. It may only be a matter of evoking a mood or of telling the audience where the dance is supposed to be taking place. These are usually the ballets with some sort of story. If you want a palace, a forest, or a lake with swans, then you really do need a designer.

Then there is the modern dance, and one thinks especially of Martha Graham, where the whole dance, the choreography, is centred upon a sculpture. It becomes part of the magnetic field of the stage in its relation to the dancers and the movement. It is part of the dance. That said, I want to turn to the actual designers. The fact is, in North America, there are very few of us at work in the lyric or musical theatre.

Our leading designer for dance is, in my opinion, Rouben Ter-Arutunian. Then comes Oliver Smith—and he is a special case. His involvement with ballet, as a director of American Ballet Theatre, is total. He not only designs but hires designers too.

Then we come to yours truly! I have a feeling they do not like to let me loose on romantic or classical ballet. But when an oddball comes along, I seem to get it.

I must mention William Pitkin, who has been a part of the Joffrey Ballet for some time and who has also worked with Ballet Theatre. My list is petering out already. Occasionally someone else is asked to do a design for dance, Bobby O'Hearn for example, but essentially we are all into opera. But, when I think of it, the list for opera is short as well.

All the major opera companies hire European designers. When it comes to major ballet productions, even with American Ballet Theatre, they usually go to Nicholas Georgiadis, Desmond Heeley or some other English designer, or perhaps to an Italian or German.

You may think a terrible injustice is being done to North American designers. But it is not as unreasonable as it seems. We have an open market. People can choose whom they will. I have a feeling it is our training that is at fault. Since teaching design at Yale, I have become very much aware of the shortcomings of North American training. Our designers do not come out of art schools. They come from theatre schools. And the fact is, our theatre schools have very little concern for opera or dance. For a long time, ballet was a dirty word in these places. It was old-fashioned, esoteric and not to be bothered with. The modern dance was more respectable, but not much so. Even the theatre history only touched on the very ancient or the very modern.

So, now you have a situation where most designers have a very limited exposure to theatre as a whole, very little appreciation for music, let alone for movement that has been married to music. Even skill in visual arts is lacking. Think of those ballets that demand a bold, flamboyant visual statement, the sort of thing in which Picasso excelled, or even Ben Shahn or Beni Montresor. Many American designers do not have that marvellous, assertive creativity. All they have been doing is learning to design interiors. Now and then somebody is a bit more advanced and gets into Brecht. Or another follows the way of Noguchi and works sculpturally. But these are very few. When they do try it is usually without a sense of the relationship of the sculptural elements to the moving bodies confined within a boxed space. What they produce then looks like a decorative piece for a bank or public building.

That is why, when the National Ballet of Canada or ABT needs a designer for one of their big productions they go where they know they will discover flair and courage, a style with a visual impact as impressive as the sound coming from the orchestra. They go, of course, to Europe.

We are not, in the true sense, producing designers, but problem-solvers and decorators. So, people ask, why not turn to the fine artists instead? That is all very well, but there is a danger. The work itself may be great but the result on stage will not necessarily be the same. Work of this kind that I have seen tends also, in the end, to be decorative, strictly a backdrop with no real relation to what else is happening on stage.

What I am saying is really a plea for better training. We have to recapture what we know to have been the creative richness of the Diaghilev period when there was a marriage of theatrical elements, when the design was not just a pretty backdrop but an integral part of the whole theatrical experience, as relevant as the music or the movement. It is also a plea for those agencies with the funds at their disposal to pay attention to this vital aspect of training designers. We have to broaden our vision of what theatre is. Then there may be a better meeting of North American designers and dance.

Ming Cho Lee's appeal for improved design training brought immediate reaction from Dame Ninette de Valois who recalled what had impressed her about the Martha Graham company during its appearance at the Royal Opera House in London (1976). "I never stopped talking about the wonderful coordination between her sets, her costumes and her dances." In England, as she explained, an attempt is being made continually among the art academies to find really good young painters to see if they can be trained to fulfil the very difficult tasks of designing for ballet. "The artist," she said, "must become a part of the theatre with the dancers, not an imposition."

Dame Ninette elaborated some of Ming Cho Lee's ideas by recounting her own early experiences in the Diaghilev Ballet Russe when she was suddenly awakened to the importance of design. Then there was a definite break between the artist-craftsman and the use of the artist, the fine artist, in the theatre.

"It was fascinating to be there and see the Picassos and the Braques and all those creative people being used for our productions. A new ballet was being put on. I think the costumes and scenery were by Braque and I know that about six of us were sitting at the back in the dresses we had to wear. We were six extremely stupid, ignorant little dancers. Diaghilev was sitting in front with his artists and other people he was talking to and we were grumbling about these dresses. Suddenly, Diaghilev lost his temper. He turned to us and simply said: "Stop thinking! If the costume does not suit you, just try to see if you can fit the costume!" Well I, being rather disciplined, was much overcome by this. I can remember the next morning creeping into the back of the theatre to have a look at the scenery and, you know, it was as if a veil had been lifted. I didn't see myself any longer, I only saw myself encased in something that was so perfectly worked out with the back-cloth. Now this was the great secret of the change in the theatre. Undoubtedly it started in the ballet world....It is so distressing the way design is taught in the theatre today. You must be an artist, you must be a painter, you must be able to feel what goes with movement. Static opera sets are quite a different problem. You've only got to look at a chorus and realize you've got something quite different. At one time, the same type of designer was used for the ballet, which of course was wrong. It was from this that Diaghilev broke entirely."

Louis Applebaum saw the problem of the artist in ballet as part of a broader problem. It is not sufficient simply to have a painter as designer, even if he understands movement. Of course one must start with craftsmanship but also be exposed to life as a total experience, read poetry, look at pictures, understand people.

"I think," explained Mr. Applebaum, "that if our educational systems would understand this better, and give those who want to live professionally in the artistic world the necessary background and impetus, as well as craftsmanship, we might be able to find the kind of people Mr. Lee and Dame Ninette are looking for."

However, Lukas Foss had misgivings about the whole direction the session on design had taken and brought it to a disquieting close. "If we are to talk about the next 25 years, then the one thing we must not do is say this is the way it's got to be done or that's the way it shouldn't be done." He felt too many invalid assumptions had been made. "Creative artists look for ideas in the garbage can. We say it's not art. They may suddenly say, well, it could be."

Mr. Foss was against drawing lines and fixing definitions. "I know my own idea of what music is changes every 10 years. By now there's almost nothing left to my old definition except that music is something that doesn't do anybody any harm."

CRITICISM

Clive Barnes

William Littler   *John Percival*

Critics, perhaps understandably, have been subjected to a great deal of abusive language, possibly more than they themselves have ever meted out to luckless artists.

However, in a forum such as that provided by the National Ballet's conference, it becomes apparent that no one is more sensitive to the shortcomings and inadequacies of the critic than the critic himself.

Here, three distinguished practitioners explain their own perceptions of how criticism may develop and improve in the next generation.

CRITICISM

Clive Barnes
The Functions of a Critic

Critics cause an incredible amount of heartburn among people who are not critics. I can understand why. It is an unfortunate name. I would prefer the more lowly title of reviewer. Do you remember Vladimir and Estragon in *Waiting for Godot*? They are screaming abuse at one another and eventually they escalate to those terrible epithets and eventually one, I forget whether it was Vladimir or Estragon, shouts out at the other, "cretin." For a moment the other tramp is completely bewildered. He cannot think of any reply. Then, suddenly, he summons up the last resources of his imagination and shouts back "critic." I think it represents to an extent a rather unfortunate and prevailing attitude.

I notice that Canada, indeed North America in general, seems unnaturally interested in critics. I was introduced today as someone who has almost become an honourary Canadian. I think that was said because you like to bait me. Last time I was here, quite recently, it was to take part in a television debate with Sir John Gielgud. It had the illuminating title "Should critics be horsewhipped?" I forget which side I was on. The time before, I was invited to go to Ottawa and then I think it was to talk about criticism. I do think that North America has far too high a regard for criticism. The English system where they swear at us but they do not admire us is much healthier.

The question of dance criticism is extraordinarily difficult. If only I had realized how difficult it was going to be in 1942, when I decided I would like to be a critic! Healthy kids want to drive fire engines. I wanted to be a critic. It really is a weird thing to want to be. I am used to doing other forms of criticism and most of it is fairly easy. But dance criticism! As I get older it doesn't get easier. It gets harder because I realize not only my individual limitations but the limitations of the entire craft. I think those limitations were extraordinarily well put by Ned Rorem, the American composer, in one of his scandalous diaries. Actually, he was writing about music, but I feel the thing is even more true of dance. He wrote: "Critics of words use words. Critics of music use words." Well if you substitute dance for music, you see what I mean.

What use are critics? I believe they serve a number of functions. First, they are the cheapest publicity the art is going to get. Sometimes it's bad news but at least people know that they are being talked about. Also, I think it does provide a fairly valuable education medium. There is very much more to what critics do than to say nasty things about last night's performance. Commentary and feature writing for example. There are many, many things that critics do which are not specifically related to any individual performance.

Dance is one of the most difficult things. How do you write about Balanchine's *Agon*? Very often we find ourselves writing about the stories, because the stories we understand. Nowadays we don't even understand the stories. They wait for us to tell them and then they deny it. But it is extraordinarily difficult. We are so often reduced to code words, hurray words, boo words. We say a dancer was "musical." What do we really mean by that? What we really mean is that he, or she, has the ability to play around with the musical phrase, take a ritard there or a slight upbeat here. Fonteyn, for example, was a superbly musical dancer. But so many of these things are intangible. How often have you read in a review that a dancer gave a "stylish" performance? Who says it was stylish? What is stylishness? We are fighting a limited vocabulary. Dance itself, at least as a widespread phenomenon, is new, especially in the English-speaking world. Before it was at best an exotic visitor. As an indigenous form it is new; and criticism is even newer.

In a way it is a wonderful time to be a critic, to be, as Edwin Denby wrote some years ago, a "new boy" at the craft. It's very experimental and great fun. But you are not going to win many prizes. Of all the critical crafts it's probaby the most shaky. Yet we do provide a valuable function. We disseminate knowledge, sometimes wrong knowledge, but knowledge. After all, the artist can always fight back and always write back if necessary. I think that critics do interest people in the dance.

I cannot help feeling that the enormous dance explosion in America (for every person in 1965 who bought a ticket for a professional show in the United States 16 bought one in 1975) is related to the phenomenon of television, not to ballet on television, but to the effects of the medium itself. It has made the younger generation much more visually oriented and therefore much more likely to enjoy a visual medium such as dance rather than a verbal medium such as theatre. This has perhaps played a part, but the support given to dance by the press has also been incredibly significant.

The first generation critics were fundamentally historians and publicists. Sometimes they were called the balletomane critics. An enormous amount of pioneer work was done by people like Cyril Beaumont and Arnold Haskell. I cannot begin to estimate how many people had their imagination sparked by Arnold Haskell's very interesting and very immediate writings on the dance. Later, as a critic, he was much criticized by younger members of his own profession. But there would not have been those younger members of his own profession had he not existed, had he not done an enormous amount of pioneering work.

In America there were people like Irving Deakin and John Martin who also did a great deal for the dance. Slowly, it was understood that there ought to be specialist critics. At one time there was no such thing as dance criticism, no such things as ballet critics; they were not particularly necessary. If such critics did exist, they were often either borrowed from

the sports desk or were the music critics. Martha
Graham always preferred sports writers. She thought
they had better eyes. Ninette de Valois always
preferred music critics. She thought that at least they
had a critical training, a critical acumen and a critical
background. But eventually the trouble with both
groups was that they made rather a lot of mistakes of
fact. Also it was awkward when it became apparent
that they often knew rather less than the general
members of the audience. So a demand arose for
specialist dance critics. I suppose we represent that
second generation; an imperfect breed, self-taught,
sometimes taught on the job, enthusiastic (sometimes
to a fault) and self-opinionated, but generally
speaking hard-working, always conscientious and very
underpaid.

We always talk about how badly dancers are
paid, but critics are even worse off. You know, in the
English-speaking world, I believe there is only one
critic who really makes a living as a dance critic.
Everyone else either has another job or a huge private
income or two critical jobs. I am a drama critic as
well as a dance critic. I did make an honest living
when I was a dance critic, just for two years, but
that's the end of that.

Now we must look to a third generation of critics
and ask ourselves where they should come from, what
they should do and what kind of relationship they
should have with the audience, with the profession
and with journalism. To talk about the future of
criticism is really a little bit like talking the future of
weather forecasting: it largely depends on the weather.
The future of dance criticism rather depends on the
dance. I do not quite know where the critics will come

from. I can conceive that a lot of them might be dancers. In my generation very few were dancers.

Notation, incidentally, may make the illiterate dance critic as unthinkable as today an illiterate music critic is. After all, you would not have a music critic who could not read a score. It depends on the strides made by notation. Ten years ago I was more confident. Now I'm not so sure.

I am doubtful whether the critics *should* come from the normal ranks of the professional dancers; personally I do not think so. I would rather have a perfectly fulfilled critic than a disappointed dancer, a disappointed choreographer or a disappointed anything else! I would much prefer to have someone who really wanted to be a critic, try to equip him or herself as a critic, and I think that equipping is best done on the audience side of the footlights. Now that is sometimes quite an unfashionable view. People will always say, "What right do you have to be a critic, could you choreograph?" "No." "Could you dance?" "Hardly." "Could you really do anything?" The answer is no. But then I am neither in the business of offering lessons in choreography, nor in the business of being a ballet master.

One of the misconceptions that dancers often harbour about critics is that they expect them to do the job that their own teachers, regisseurs and ballet masters should do. They do not get the right kind of correction in many companies. At least, so it seems. That is not really what the critic is all about. The critic is there to build a bridge between the audience and the artist, to make the artist's job that little bit easier. Obviously he is at times going to be judgmental; he is obviously going to be prejudiced.

There is no such thing as objective criticism. This is one of the most dangerous fallacies. You sometimes find it in North America. People think that they are right. We have too many critics who either think they are Moses or think they are the person delivering the news to Moses. This is a most unfortunate attitude for critics to take. They are entirely subjective. They may be wrong. They are advocates, not judges. They are advocates, obviously, for their own prejudices. This is a very important point that we must try very hard to instil into the new generation of critics.

Another thing I notice in North America is that we have dozens and dozens of critics. It's a very, very curious situation. In 1965, I was brought from England to the *New York Times* (shrieking and screaming I must admit) and the reason was that at the time, in my age group, there just was not a suitable North American critic. Had I remained in England, with only two or three exceptions, I would still be the youngest English dance critic, which is unfortunate for England. In North America, I find I am almost a grand old man apart from about two or three older ones such as Walter Terry or Ann Barzel in Chicago. We have in North America an incredible number of people who want to be critics. They are enthusiastic about it; they are violent about it. What worries me a little is that when my generation, the second generation of critics, came up, certainly we were cheeky, we were rude, we were irreverent, but we had to a certain extent done our homework. We had seen an enormous amount of dance.

When I started to write, I had been to dance consistently for about eight to ten years. I had seen a terrific amount and although I probably only knew about a tenth of what I thought I knew, and about a fifth of what I hoped I knew, at least I did have a fairly considerable background not only in my native companies but also in others across the world. When I started, at least I had the confidence of my own arrogance. I now find writers who have no background. One young lady, a few years ago, was proposing to write about a whole season of the Bolshoi Ballet without actually ever having seen the company. This is all very enthusiastic but rather disturbing, because if you go and review a Swan Lake, and it is the first Swan Lake you have ever seen, I hasten to point out that it is not only the best goddamn Swan Lake you have ever seen, it is also the worst goddamn Swan Lake you have ever seen! I would like to see such people pause a little before rushing into public print.

Another thing I see in North America and the English-speaking world generally, a very disturbing thing, concerns the development of critics. If, as I believe, this involves seeing as wide and as varied a spectrum of dance as possible, then (I hate to say this) probably only New York and London can provide the proper breeding grounds. Nowadays perhaps you could add Washington and Toronto, and those two cities in part because of their proximity to New York. Dance is not the kind of thing you can study in front of a television, a cinema screen or a stereo; it is not enough to read about it. Dance has actually to be seen on the stage. A film critic is much better off. They are so lucky. A 19-year-old film buff can have seen, in its original version, as it were, every film he needs to set himself up as a critic. He will be a very pushy little sapient; I've met a lot of them. But on the other hand, he *will* have acquired the experience. It is even a little better for drama critics. I remember when Kenneth Tynan was about 18 or 19, his knowledge of the theatrical repertory was daunting. Now in dance, we just cannot do that.

Lastly, do remember, the critics to an extent have a duty as the custodians of tradition. Dame Ninette talked about tradition and I like to think that the custodians, the critics, do help in this. We tend to be very zealous in guarding the things we remember from childhood. It is probably a sign of instant decrepitude and oncoming menopause, but we do. I am still offended, for example, when I see James in *La Sylphide* do a complete double turn in the second act when he should do a one and a half. Sometimes critics may seem very pernickety, especially when their memory is fading them. On the other hand, they do care about such things, they do care about traditions.

There is something else I would wish for the third generation critics, the ones who are going to replace me and dance on my grave—and some of them have started doing it prematurely. I hope they will remember their position as a link between artists and audience, and I hope they and the dance companies will have much closer links. This is a difficult matter. The critic occupies a strange position in the profession. Some of my best friends are dancers. Some of my best friends are even directors. Some of my *worst* friends are directors! Still, I think some contact is helpful. The critic has information and knowledge. Sometimes he can give advice. The danger, of course, is taking the critic's advice!

I always remember Lucia Chase coming to me once, saying she wanted a cheap little Massine ballet, a *ballet bouffe*, and she couldn't think of one; what did I think would be a good idea? I said the Joffrey had had a *Beau Danube*, and *Tricorne* would cost too much. Why not try *Gaîté Parisienne*? I think I even suggested where she could get the decor and costumes cheap. She said it was a marvellous idea and did it—a disaster! I remember starting my notice, "I can't imagine what idiot suggested to Ballet Theatre...."

Critics should take great care to discover and monitor ongoing company policies. In a sense, the dance companies are public properties and should be publicly accountable. Nobody is going to raise questions in Parliament or in the Senate about how George Balanchine or Alexander Grant is running his company. Really, the critic is the only person in a public position who can. The companies, understandably enough, do not always like it, but critics must concern themselves with issues of dance policy. They have to be part reviewer, part political commentator and part ombudsman. Who else is going to point out that ticket prices are soaring unreasonably or that the box office is being rude to people or the ushers are kicking people in the aisles? Who is going to point out that someone is building a theatre with a concrete stage and no sight lines? The role of the critic must be taken as a public role in every way. I hope the third generation will be better informed than my generation was, more able to handle this kind of thing. I hope they will have a better historical perspective. They will not have to do the job of educating a public that the first generation had. They will not have to worry about the acceptance of dance; only about the dance itself. They will be much more full-fledged critics, in the way music or literary critics are. I look forward to that day.

Most of all, I hope the next 25 years will be as much fun for them as the past 25 years have been for me. It has been a fantastic time; I really loved almost every minute of it. I have the valuable critical ability of liking bad ballets more than most people like good ballets. It is a useful thing, which I recommend to the aspiring critic.

A final word to the third generation. Realize that you are not pariahs. When you give people bad notices, they will not like you, but they will as soon as you start giving them good notices again. Just be as fair as possible.

Someone once asked a quite well-known choreographer in New York whether she did not think it awful that Clive Barnes hated her so much. She replied, "Hate me? He doesn't hate me at all. He loves me. It's just my ballets he can't stand." That is one of the nicest things that was ever said about me and epitomizes an attitude that critics should very much take to heart.

William Littler

Dance Criticism in Canada

Critics are notoriously bad fortune tellers. It is difficult enough for us to get our facts straight about last night's performance, much less anticipate the next 25 years. If it's the future of ballet we are concerned with here, then more reliable information can be obtained from some turbanned matron with an ample supply of tea leaves. Yet it does seem to me that unless we are to follow the biblical admonition to consider the lillies, we ought to take some thought for tomorrow, if only because we are told that those who fail to benefit from history's lessons are consigned to repeat them.

If we take a look at the history of ballet criticism in this country, we can find much that might be called mistaken. Since our period of anticipation is 25 years, let's begin by looking back 25 years, to 1951 and the first reviews written of the National Ballet of Canada. Excerpts from them are hanging even now in the lobby of the O'Keefe Centre here in Toronto. They are encouraging, brief and are written by non-specialists. Of course, we can hardly expect the reviews of 1951 to have been written by what one might describe as professional dance critics. There was not enough professional dance in any Canadian city to sustain one. With the National Ballet just beginning, Les Grands Ballets Canadiens not yet born and the Winnipeg Ballet neither Royal nor especially active, the reviewer had to subsist on one-night-stands by the Ballet Russe de Monte Carlo, Ballet Theatre or similar touring organizations that ventured an occasional toe into "the true north, strong and free."

So the reviews were generally written by people who spent most of their time doing other things.

Some of these people at least were professional reviewers, some of them did not know a bourrée from a donkey. But 1976 is very different from 1951 as far as dance is concerned in Canada. In Toronto there are times in which it is possible to chose from among five different performances and the country as a whole is helping to support nearly three dozen dance companies.

As for our three major ballet companies, they have all toured internationally, and have matured to the point where they can be described as important national institutions. The dancers are professionals, the choreographers are professionals, the productions they mount are professional and the reviews, well, in most cases, the reviews are still written by non-professionals. I'd go even further than that, I'd say there's no such thing as a profession of dance criticism in Canada.

Now before I become any more rabid on this subject, perhaps I had better explain what I mean by dance criticism, because I do not feel it's synonymous with dance reviewing. We have always had dance reviewing, ever since Champlain's inebriated fellow members of the Order of Good Cheer stumbled through their first evening's entertainment on the shores of Acadia. A dance reviewer, I take it, is someone sent to write a dance review. He may be a civilized human being, but when asked to state his credentials, he really need not say any more than Stanley Kauffman did when asked the same question: "I am a writer." A critic is more than a writer. Criticism is a branch of aesthetics and proceeds from a philosophy of art. The critic is someone with a broad historical knowledge of the art to which he addresses himself and some working hypotheses about its nature. The dance critic knows the literature from Noverre to Kirstein and beyond and he has a grasp of the vocabulary of ballet, the choreographic process, the nature of movement: he is a very rare bird! But, by virtue of his critical equipment, he is able to put the particular dance event into a general picture and it's the larger picture that we've been missing in Canadian dance writing. We have plenty of reactions to specific events but relatively little appreciation of how they relate to the growth of a choreographer, a company, an art. And this is what I hope to see develop in the next 25 years. It is not really so much. It is really no more than inviting dance writers to become thoughtful and educated in the same way other dance professionals are.

Newspapers still appoint instant dance critics. Magazines still feel that ballet must be written about in terms of the dancers' off-stage life. There is a widespread reluctance to take a serious art seriously. So I charge those of you who want criticism to do something about it. In saying this, I am reminded of what Somerset Maugham wrote in *Of Human Bondage.* "People ask you for criticism, but they only want praise." If you only want praise, you are doing yourselves as dancers, choreographers and viewers a severe injustice. You have before you in the National Ballet an institution that has grown up. You have around you in public print and on the airwaves, commentators on that institution who are themselves still in their critical adolescence. Perhaps by the year 2001 we will have begun to shave. At this point, I crave your indulgence if I wax pseudo-Churchillian and say, "Give us the razor and we'll do the shave," because I know some of you believe that those of us who review ballets are always in possession of a razor. In fact, most of us operate with blunt instruments. I am going to leave this metaphor now before I get into any deeper lather.

It is somehow universally expected that a critic

should be a self-made man, that he should learn by osmosis. I think there is some truth to that belief and I would subscribe to Clive Barnes' view that a person ought ideally to have seen a great deal of ballet before he starts writing about it. At the same time it would be naïve of the dance community to make provision for the training of dancers and choreographers and assume that the people who try to inform the public about their work do not themselves need an education more sophisticated than mere osmosis. Something is needed. It's time for the critic to become as much a professional as the artist he views and reviews. That's a task that may well take us the next 25 years.

John Percival

The Critic's Responsibility

Somebody once asked Martha Graham what was the future of modern dance. She answered, "If I knew what was the future of modern dance, I wouldn't tell a soul. I'd go ahead and do it myself." Happily I do not know what is the future of dance criticism or of dance itself over the next 25 years. But I think one can see a few pointers to the way things *might* develop. From time to time during this conference we have talked about the effect of videotaping, about what video can do for dancers. There is also the question of what video can do for critics.

At the moment the critic has an awful problem because, for the most part, he is writing for people who have not seen what he is writing about. In Britain we have a satirical magazine called *Private*

Eye that has a feature called Pseuds Corner in which they reprint what are thought to be the most outrageously funny remarks from the newspapers. I have only twice had the honour of appearing in Pseuds Corner. On each occasion it was not for any outrageous opinion I might have expressed; it was simply because I tried to describe as accurately as possible what happened on stage. Obviously, on occasion people did not believe me. A great many things in criticism could be much simplified if only we could show rather than tell. That might be a possibility for the future.

For the moment, as my colleagues have said, we are all self-trained, self-taught people. Incidentally, it is not only the sports writers and the music writers who have dealt with criticism in the past. I discovered recently that when the Diaghilev Ballet first came to London, some of their performances were reviewed for the *Times* by the paper's military correspondent. But if we are all self-taught, then we are really only in the same position as the pioneers of modern dance, who have had to go out and make their own technique. Perhaps the critics of the future will be trained like ballet dancers.

In North America now it is possible to have some training as a dance critic. That is not true of Europe at all. It may mean that people, who would make good dance critics if self-taught, acquire their craft and their skill much quicker. On the other hand, I see dangers in this. Some of the young writers in America, whom I see coming up with marvellous theories, start their reviews with the theories and then, about three-quarters of the way through an article, suddenly try to relate them to a performance they have seen. It does not work or help anyone connected with the performance. It does not help anyone to understand anything about dance at all.

As Clive Barnes has said, the future of criticism depends largely on the future of ballet and none of us can really tell for sure what is going to happen there. Twenty-five years ago Canadian ballet was still an infant, kicking and squealing in its cradle, and ballet in Britain and the United States was something of a gawky adolescent.

Over the last 25 years, the two biggest influences we have seen have been the influx of ideas from Russia, which until 20-odd years ago was very much a closed book to the rest of the world as far as dance was concerned, and also the growing relationship between classical ballet and modern dance. I know Dame Ninette de Valois disagrees, but I think they have had a very beneficial effect on one another and have grown, valuably, much closer together. It's in the nature of art to develop by contrasts and changes. I suspect one of the things that is going to happen over the next 25 years is that having grown closer together, they are now going to start drifting a lot more apart. The modern dance people, the young modern dance choreographers, are already becoming much more puristic in their art, much more determined to do something which is not only unlike classical ballet but unlike anything any modern dancer has ever done. Equally classical ballet, having assimilated many valuable ideas from modern dance, is now going to say, "Enough," and concentrate on its roots for a while, using its new-found expressiveness with much more strictness to its classical background.

One change that may come about, that has

perhaps already started to come about and which in my mind *should* come about, was hinted at earlier. It is the matter of the mature dancers. What is to happen to them? One answer is that many more mature dancers ought to be on stage; they are retiring far too early. We have ballet troupes in which the entire population of the company is like the inhabitants of a new suburb, full of young newly-married couples with no older people at all. What kind of relationship to real life can the choreographers produce if their raw material consists only of good-looking young people?

There has been a recent tendency for dance to accept that somebody who is thin can dance, that somebody who is fat, somebody who is tall or short, even somebody who is getting old can dance, and can dance well and has something valuable to contribute to the scene. If ballet over the next 25 years can manage to enlarge its raw material in this way, to realize that dancing is not something that you confine to one physique, one age group, one kind of look, then it will enrich itself greatly.

However, the reason we cannot see very far ahead to the way dance will develop is because so much of it depends on who comes along to do it. Earlier, Dame Ninette de Valois defined very valuably three meanings of style in ballet. I would say there is a fourth sense—personal style. To some extent that is true of the dancer who must come over on stage as a person who is *conveying* something, about whom one would say, if we saw him in ordinary life, he's got style. We don't just mean that they are nicely dressed or that they carry themselves well, or that they've got a strong personality. What we mean is that everything relates together, everything is part of an understanding of what the person wants from life, what the person wants to do in life. This is even more important in choreographers: it's the personal style of choreographers that is going to make the difference.

There has been much talk about the shortage of choreographers in Canada. It is not an exclusively Canadian problem but is true almost everywhere in the world, except perhaps in Holland which, although only a small country with a very new ballet tradition, has already produced at least three rather distinguished choreographers. The fact is, shortage or no, it is when the choreographer of genius and imagination appears that we will get real changes in the dance.

What part can critics play when all this is happening? As has already been pointed out, the job of criticism is not just a matter of judging things. It is not only a matter of popularizing. (We all know the well-known theatrical fact that if a ballet or play or any other kind of show is a flop, it was "killed" by the critics. If it is a success, that of course was entirely on its own merits.) The critics can play some little part in helping the deserving things that are developing to become more widely known and to become more widely understood. There is still an educative part for the critic to play. It just strikes me—there has been talk of the great ballet explosion in North America since 1965. Of course 1965 was the year Clive Barnes came to New York, so one could say that's the cause of it all.

Another thing critics do is to record the present. In effect, it is the critics of the past who are valuable to today's dancers, choreographers and audiences in providing some knowledge of what happened in the past. Yet, when I look at the newspapers after a premiere and see what some of my colleagues have written, I wonder what kind of record it is of the past!

Also, a critic must try to remember and to draw attention to what's in danger of being forgotten. When we go on nagging ballet companies for not doing this, that and the other, it is not just a matter of *tours en l'air* in *La Sylphide*; it is something rather bigger than that. There cannot be any kind of improvement and development without a choice. If you go down *this* road, you make a choice not to go down *that* road. Fine, but there comes a time when the critic has got to say, in going along a certain line of development, you are in danger of losing something you used to have. Do you want to lose that altogether or do you want to go back and pick that up? Equally, the critic should be able to point out what is happening in the other arts.

Clive Barnes' suggestion, that North America is perhaps too preoccupied with its critics, was partly borne out by the barrage of questions that followed his and his colleagues' presentations. To an extent, these had all thrown doubt on the reliability of newspaper reviewing and criticism generally. As Clive Barnes put it: "Never believe a critic." But are there ways in which the innocent reader can protect himself against shoddy criticism?

John Percival felt there was a general and false underestimation of the intelligence of readers. If one follows a particular critic's writing consistently, even without having seen the performances in question, the reader develops a sensitivity to that critic's knowledge and prejudices. "The bad critic is eventually going to show himself up." Of course, as he went on to explain, the best reviews—the ones hardest to write—do not state opinions but imply them by the very manner, tone or style in which they describe what actually occurred on stage.

Given the less than satisfactory state of dance criticism, what could be done to improve it? The panelists could not agree among themselves that a formal system of grants to aspiring critics would improve the situation. It would seem an odd reversal of priorities to divert funds from the artists themselves to cultivate the people who were going to criticize them. Both Clive Barnes and John Percival recounted the difficult early days of their writing careers when they had to slip into a theatre during an intermission or buy the cheapest seats simply in order to expand their knowledge of the dance repertoire.

Mr. Barnes thought the companies themselves could help by allotting complimentary seats to any bright young aspiring critics who appear. In fact, they should look out for them. There was certainly general agreement on one point. Critics, aspiring or arrived, had a duty to maintain broad cultural horizons, immersing themselves in as many of the arts as possible. Without this breadth of vision, their contribution to the art of dance would be poor indeed.

It was clear from a number of the questions that the audience was unhappy with much of the criticism and reviews they read. What could readers do and what should newspapers do?

Clive Barnes explained the difficulty facing the management of small daily papers. There simply is not enough material to warrant hiring a full-time dance critic. The choice is then between employing a journalist with a roving commission as reviewer, critic and feature writer, or of employing freelance writers who are experts in their particular fields. This latter would be the best course and newspapers should search out reliable freelancers.

As for the readers, they should make their voices heard by writing to the newspapers when they object to material. William Littler thought it was as important for the critic to hear when he had done something right as it was to hear when he had done something wrong. He very much regretted the reluctance of the average reader to write to the editor of a paper. If, as Clive Barnes had described, the critic was a bridge between the artist and the audience, then there should be some form of contact between the critic and the public he serves.

Perhaps improvement in writing would accompany the growing availability of formal instruction in criticism at universities and colleges. However, no amount of training can substitute for the vital element that a successful critic must have, what Clive Barnes called "critical acumen." After that, the critic must discipline himself to acquire the other technical attributes of his most difficult profession.

FUNDING

Peter Brinson
Timothy Porteous

Although it may not yet have reached the almost impossible costliness of opera, ballet requires a great deal of money if it is to have those elements that lend it artistic distinction and popular appeal.

It is very proper that ballet dancers should at last be receiving a subsistence. However, their salaries, added to the prohibitive costs of production, (especially for new ballets), adds up to a very large sum—the source of much concern to boards of directors and to managers.

Although the situation is indeed grave, both Peter Brinson and Timothy Porteous (each senior administrative figures in funding organizations that have been notably generous to the ballet) offer some advice, encouragement and hope for the future.

FUNDING

Peter Brinson
A Bigger Future

The Nature of the Problem
In the autumn of 1976, the Australian government's
Industrial Assistance Commission handed down a
report that rocked the Australian cultural scene. It
recommended the elimination, over five years, of all
subsidy to major opera, ballet and drama companies,
reducing by 20% each year. The Australian federal
government said it would not act on the report but
this did not allay company fears. Anyway, that is not
quite the point. Economic recession in Australia, as
elsewhere, has brought about a rethinking of priorities
in every aspect of government policy. The process has
dictated value judgements that in this case suggested
not dismantling the companies so much as reassessing
the relevance of what they are doing in order to see if
their activities are not merely lulling middle-class
audiences into a deeper complacence. The

Commission, in its own rough way, asked the companies to have a long, hard think about the nature of their service to the Australian people and, as one Australian writer elegantly put it, "to find some way to get new bums on their subsidized seats, bums that don't come from the same affluent suburbs."

I begin in this way because I think the challenge presented by that Australian Commission, including the origin and number of bums on seats, is the challenge that must be faced. We should face, too, the controversy that influenced the Commission's thinking and that still divides all funding policies in advanced industrial countries today. Are we for the democratization of culture or for cultural democracy? The term "democratization of culture" means the bringing of heritage culture to the greatest number of people, recognizing that this remains still a minority of the population. Cultural democracy, by contrast, means using our limited funds for the majority of the population to stimulate the spirit of creativity, which many people passionately believe lies somewhere deep inside every human being.

There are a number of other related challenges we have to face common to all our Western capitalist democracies: the enormous lag of cultural awareness still to be overcome in every population; the crisis of communication between artist, politician and business man that results in artists, including dancers, being seen as something apart from society—never in Parliament, never in the policy-making echelons of society, as unsure of their place in society as society is of them—with all that this means in society's unwillingness to support any funding priority. Thus

we have the general poverty of primary creative
artists, often living below recognized poverty levels.
There is, too, a need everywhere for fact-gathering for
statistics, and a reliable assessment of the effects of
funding; a need for international collaboration in
developing certain resources, such as the fostering of
choreographers. There is the potent, but inadequately
explored, link between art and education, each a
resource for the other. But, greater than any other
problem, the economic situation in all countries
everywhere invites, as it has done in Australia, a
radical rethinking of cultural policy, and dance policy
within it. The problem of funding, therefore, involves
fundamental policy decisions for the next 25 years.
Yet it can be fairly simply presented. Whether one is
considering national policy or the particular problems
of one company, funding falls naturally into two
parts.

First is the actual money bit—the economics.
Second, and much larger, is the element of
communication—the projection of your case, in this
instance the case for dance, to the rest of society.
Without communication there is no money. So, I shall
look first and briefly at economics; then at
communication; then draw some conclusions for the
future. What I cannot offer is a magic formula to
solve all company funding worries. There is no such
formula in the real world.

Economics

A look then, at money. Let's begin with the
international scene. I have checked and expanded
some figures from 1975 showing Canada fourth in the
league of per capita expenditure on the arts after West
Germany, Sweden and Austria. Compared with its

American neighbour, Canada has not done badly but it would be misleading to look simply at the total figures spent on dance by the Canada Council and America's National Endowment for the Arts. The American agency's budget includes an item missing in its Canadian counterpart, a sizeable disbursement for education in the arts. It is a matter we shall return to later.

What the figures do show is that what has been achieved in Canada over the last 25 years has been done on a minute sum, which speaks volumes for the courage, breadth and originality of Canadian funding and arts institutions. At the same time this rather small proportion of the national budget—which is just as small in most other industrial capitalist countries—goes a long way toward explaining the chronic crisis in which the performing arts find themselves. The extent of the crisis needs emphasizing because society as a whole doesn't understand, or ignores, the nature of the problem.

Being labour intensive—labour being both input and output—there is no way in the performing arts that technical progress can raise the productivity of labour sufficient to cover necessary increases in costs and salaries. This fact needs to be driven home to politicians and administrators because, unless they grasp it, the arts will grow poorer and poorer. How do you raise the productivity of a dancer? You can't. So any increase in costs must be wholly inflationary, resulting either in seat price inflation (and empty houses) or the growing gap we all face between income and expenditure.

One result of the inflationary crisis has been to create a relatively new academic subject, the economics of the arts. It exists to some extent on studying the obvious, but postulates a quite useful law, that because of their labour intensity, the performing arts, along with certain other services like education, must steadily and cumulatively outstrip the rate of inflation in the rest of the country. This grim law explains the ever more difficult decisions facing artistic boards, audiences and fund raisers. Budgets, including the contingency account, need not only to keep pace with inflation, but also to outstrip it by ever wider margins if companies are not to go bankrupt.

It is tempting to argue that the explanation of this problem in such detached academic terms excuses companies who cannot make ends meet. Alas, it is not so. It does not remove from artistic boards responsibility for finance, nor for the selection of policy options and priorities that go with that responsibility. Since it is in the selection of these options and priorities that the quality of a board and a president reveals itself, the financial crisis tends merely to separate good sheep from bad goats. What should the beleaguered boards do? They could turn again to the academic world for another helpful "explanation." In return they might be referred to a science called Cost Benefit Analysis, which is fairly young in the arts.

The great joy of Cost Benefit Analysis is that it attempts to provide a measure of justification for expenditures that are not commercially viable. So this is the first step to a subdivision of the economics of the arts into a branch that actually studies deficit-producing activities. In turn, this goes some way to providing a weapon—or at least a shield—with which companies can face critical politicians and business leaders. Since we live in a profit-oriented society, many people, especially those in business and government, are inclined to panic over loss-making operations.

Panic not, say the economists, because we have not only Cost Benefit Analysis but Cost Effectiveness Analysis and other ingenious concepts to show that profit is not what you thought it was. It is much more than just spare money. It provides also the social *justification* of expenditure and the social *measure* of its effectiveness.

Thus profit has to be gauged in social terms as well as financial terms. If there is no profit in either sense, the expenditure has been wasted, but if there is profit, or anticipated profit, the expenditure is justified. Which leads to the next question of *how much* expenditure (i.e. subsidy) and so to arts economist Keith Diggle's definition of subsidy as "the sum of money needed to support an operation when the maximum number of people are using the service and paying as much as their individual circumstances will allow."

I know that such a definition drastically over-simplifies the nature of subsidy and makes no allowance for priorities, but at least it is a guide that takes into account the very special peculiarity of arts economics, that supply creates demand. Note again, too, that this shield does not excuse companies from those marketing activities at which they are often not very good—product planning, research and development, market research, test marketing, advertising, sales promotion and so on. My point in drawing attention to academic economics, therefore, is that company administrators and arts administrators generally need to be much more aware than they are of the field of economic theory growing up behind the practice of public and private subsidy. They need to know how to use this theory and this thinking when required to answer the kind of questions that government—or my own foundation—always asks: how, which, what, why, when, where and who?

Such knowledge can help reduce deficits and persuade grant-giving organizations, especially government, that arts enterprises have a sense of responsibility even though they remain unprotected from the economic law that sees them steadily and cumulatively outstripping the rate of inflation in the rest of the economy. The academic argument for Cost Benefit Analysis even indicates the direction of salvation—not, of course, in its updating of the social profit element, which is as old as Adam Smith, but rather in the way it suggests that all of us, alongside our struggle with daily economics, need to do what the Australian Industrial Assistance Commission was requiring of Australian companies—justify our place in the economy and our service to the nation. This doesn't preclude *us* asking politicians and others to get their thinking straight and stop expecting the wrong kind of profit from our operations.

Seen in this light, the struggle for funding faces each of us with a double task, the two parts of funding. First the business of estimates, budgetary control, planning, market research, sales promotion and so on: the day-to-day, sometimes boring, always difficult duties of a president, a board and company administration serving artistic policy. This policy, too, must satisfy several tests. For example, it must develop and retain the company's own individual image, no matter what the subsidy problems, and it must capture the public through quality rather than quantity in repertory and dancers. This part of funding, therefore, turns on how to use inadequate funds to the best advantage. We are speaking, in fact, of management and accountancy skills, even legal skills, which the dance world rarely commands. The dance world needs to use the professions and the universities much more than it does, while the universities and professions, on their side, need to study the special needs of dance administration within the overall subject of arts management. In practice this means arguing the case not only for arts management studies at, say, at least one institute for higher education in every Canadian province, but for a dance administration option within such studies.

Even so, the best dance administration, the most eloquent approaches to federal, local and private funding bodies, the greatest skill in making a little go a long way, all this is short term, a ritual that cannot provide a long-term solution to our problem. We stave off disaster this year to face fresh disaster next year.

Will we still be moving through this cycle 25 years hence? The answer lies in the way our dance world—in concert with the rest of the arts—approaches the second part of the funding problem, the factor of *communication*. First, in the field of policy; second, in the field of education.

Communication

Policy first! The dance world as a whole, and Canadian dance individually, has not come to terms with the need to argue its case collectively at the

Parliamentary bar of our technological society. Simply, the problem is how to induce a greater flow from the money taps—federal taps, provincial and local government taps, foundation taps and business taps—at a time when many other areas need irrigating while the flow itself is reduced. The real problem is not money at all, but priorities, and therefore politics. The real problem is how to demonstrate that dance is worth a very high priority in our cultural, social, educational, and political thinking—the very question posed by the Australian Commission about service to the nation!

Some members of the dance profession have shown a special genius for advocating the case of dance in government circles. Their particular institutions have benefitted accordingly. But I do not think this can be said of the dance profession generally. By and large, we are not good at projecting the profession to the nation or at thinking through the influence of social and technological change upon the collective practice of dance, and the response that dance ought to make. Hence the great significance of this conference. It rightly celebrates not just the National Ballet's 25 years, but a record of *collective* achievement by all Canadian dance companies in each of the five areas at which government funding policy usually aims:

1.) Diffusion geographically across the country
2.) Diffusion vertically among new audiences
3.) Maintaining and raising artistic standards
4.) Encouraging new forms and new artists
5.) Developing the arts in a community sense, which some people call community arts.

From this description of traditional funding areas, we can abstract the specific tasks that have faced each individual dance company since the beginning:

1.) Regular major city seasons
2.) Regular visits to smaller towns and cities
3.) Building an informed public in various styles of dance
4.) Building an interest in live theatre through school performance; lecture demonstrations; workshops for children and adults; audience involvement through "friends" and associations; publicity; and a measure of work in the community.

This is where we are now. But inevitably the inheritance has also created certain conflicts. The resolution of these conflicts is a task for the future. Most obvious is that between building new audiences and reaching new areas. Ostensibly, both aims will be achieved through extensive touring and the provision of as many new regional centres as possible. Actually, so far as audience-building is concerned, touring is a very short-term policy with a relatively short-term impact, whereas the provision of regional centres, while slower, produces more permanent results. Touring tends to satisfy immediate demand. It is more politically attractive and so usually wins in the inevitable competition for funds. There tends to be a conflict between satisfying current demand and the need for building potential demand. Even so, the tasks of geographical diffusion and audience diffusion both need local participation and local provision. The ultimate emphasis of national funding policy to achieve these ends *must* be on regional and local development—a shift common to every industrial country with experience of public subsidy. Ultimately, the conflict between the relatively short-term needs of an audience diffusion policy and the longer-term needs of regional development is reduced to the best use of available resources—not just cash, but dance companies, dancing teachers and so on—a need, in fact, to assess the past and plan for the future.

Looking at the problem this way reveals how the arts world in general, and the splintered dance world in particular, lack the policy review machinery available to other spending areas such as the sciences and education. There are, I know, periodic policy reviews carried out by arts councils at all levels, but these are usually short-term projections, perhaps over five years. They do not command the resources needed to think further ahead and to produce the persuasive policy papers that influence governments.

To fill this gap in Britain, and perhaps in the Commonwealth, my own foundation is allotting a proportion of its resources to provide a "think-tank" for the arts in the broadest sense. Initially, a series of national policy reviews studying specific fields has been undertaken. This is not an expensive undertaking—thinking never is—but it needs to be seen to be independent, so one result from this conference ought to be an approach to some Canadian foundation to see if it cannot establish a similar central policy review machinery at least for dance if not for all the arts. It should be charged not only with the task of policy review, but also with attracting the best brains from professional and academic resources appropriate to each task under the guidance of a small central administration. Artistic excellence, alas, is not enough by itself today. We need also its projection into financial and social policy. Such projection can be achieved properly only on the basis of adequate information.

Other lessons from the past 25 years of Canadian experience reinforce the need for such a "think-tank" to help place arts funding on a more rational, permanent basis. The achievement of these years has been to establish the political and social case for funding, to create the institutions of funding such as arts councils and the Canada Council itself. A highly desirable diversity of funding has been attained, but this diversity implies some measure of coordination. This in turn implies also the need for an overall cultural policy embracing recreational, leisure and arts facilities at every level with periodic examinations of the functions of the institutions concerned—including dance institutions—to prevent the growth of entrenched interests, to challenge established views and, now that they are 25 years old, perhaps to broaden and rethink the functions of these institutions.

If, too, the national characteristic of Canada is diversity, which it is, such a rethinking must surely give special attention to the unique ability of dance in Canada to reflect the diversity of Canada's peoples locally while at the same time translating this diversity into other forms that express Canadianism nationally. The arts, but dance especially, can give Canadian expression and a Canadian image to those "forces of geography" that troubled the writers of the Massey Report 25 years ago and are likely still to trouble Canadians 25 years hence. This is why I argued in my report on professional training that such a unique quality provides strong cause for special

encouragement to dancing at each political level of
Canadian life.

Canadian experience is not, however, gained in
isolation from the rest of the world. It reflects and
contributes to international experience, especially in
matters such as the devolution of the arts where there
are particular Canadian practices from which other
nations may learn. Theories and practices of
devolution currently occupy the thoughts of artists
and administrators in most advanced industrial
countries. In Britain, for example, the Redcliffe-Maud
report devoted a good deal of space to this, correctly
identifying the local government and education sectors
as funding growth points for the arts over the next
decade, notwithstanding present economic problems.
Yet devolution, in a country such as Canada, gives
rather special significance to national audience
diffusion policies because unless diffusion is
successful, devolution of the arts cannot be viable.
This in turn means breaking the middle-class image
that ballet in particular seems to have acquired.

If we attempt to do this, will there be a conflict
between the constant need to maintain and raise
standards, including audience appreciation standards,
and the cost of attracting new audiences—not just
financial cost, but the effort in terms of dancers and
repertory, of devising new or special presentation
methods? Actually, we have no choice: the effort
must be made. Otherwise we may become embroiled
in the argument that subsidy should be redistributed
from large and therefore expensive companies and
institutions to community arts enterprises where
supposedly it can benefit more people at the grass
roots level.

This argument is valid only if companies, and artists generally, were to concentrate on serving their own established audience while ignoring other audience possibilities. Whatever the achievements made already through subsidy, its total value is still inadequate in national terms. It begs the question to turn the problem into an internal conflict. The argument for redistribution is false on another count.

Because standards tend to be set by traditional arts little appreciated by the broad mass of people it does not follow, even in class terms, that concepts of quality are irrelevant or that there should be no discrimination between good and bad. Standards are certainly easier to talk about than to define but cultural democracy does not imply low standards. Rather, it means that many people denied a chance to enjoy the arts should be helped to approach them primarily through participation in creative activity. It means taking every available step to open to everyone opportunities to see and enjoy the performing arts as a stimulus to participation and an example of standards.

Whatever the approach, the concept of cultural democracy is here to stay and has important social implications for the dancing profession. Experience suggests, for example, that in every western country the dancing profession is too self-centred and inward-looking. Our profession needs to be more concerned, and to be seen to be more concerned, about service to the nation and the communities within it. Dance cannot be successful in getting the financial support it needs from the public unless the public feels some service is being provided. By the public, I mean not just a middle-class public but workers and young people for whom it is real hardship to find the price of a ticket, and who therefore need to be approached as well as attracted. Hence the need for a whole new kind of educational and community dance service not separate from the big companies but linked to them and nourished by them. The key to this is education, to which I will return, but education needs to be supported and perhaps even anticipated by a rethinking of box-office priorities if the culturally or economically disadvantaged are to be attracted. In turn, this requires an allocation of subsidy for social purposes designed not necessarily to secure maximum cash takings (i.e. maximum profit), but to achieve minimum unsatisfied demand. Therefore box-office prices should primarily be commensurate with a high use of capacity. This implies, in turn, schemes of positive discrimination to favour particular types of audiences, usually through a voucher system, which can include some transport subsidy for people out of town.

Any such step is likely to be ineffective without a monitoring and research service to analyze audiences and help in the formulation of policy to reach new audiences. Head counting is not enough because an increase in audience may simply reflect a larger audience from the same affluent group. An effective audience policy needs to know the frequency of attendance, age, education, occupation and distance travelled, as well as the level of family income. The research necessary could be a function of the "think-tank" already suggested, or be provided by a separate body specially established. It might even be an additional responsibility of the government statistical service or perhaps be undertaken by the private sector of business.

The idea that business might take such an initiative is almost unthinkable in Europe because there business sponsorship of the arts has never become as significant as it is in North America. I make the suggestion here because the business community is genuinely a third partner with the federal and local government in the funding process and because many great artistic institutions on this side of the Atlantic, including the National Ballet of Canada, owe their inception to the initiative of the private sector. Nevertheless, the last 25 years offer certain lessons for this sector too, reflected already in the responsible initiatives of the Canadian Council for Business and the Arts. The contributions of industrial sponsors to the arts, however important, should never be regarded as a substitute or alternative to public spending. Some agreed code of sponsorship is needed so that the well-being and artistic freedom of the artist is not threatened, or is not bought by money. A principle of "industrial responsibility" should be established whereby certain industries are required to make a financial contribution to the well-being of the art forms that contribute to their prosperity. Advertising should help the visual arts, television, the performing arts, and so on. Because of the importance of the work place in the lives of working people, industry should do more in conjunction with trade unions to provide for art activities in work places and arts sponsorships in local communities near the factory.

The tendency of sponsorship money is to go to the prestigious arts, which often need it least. A percentage of business sponsorship money, therefore, should go to a central fund to support the experimental, community and "fringe" arts that are often the creative seeds of tomorrow.

Business need not restrict its help to giving money. It can offer financial expertise, management and administrative know-how. It might be worth considering for Canada an organization similar to the Action Resource Centre (A.R.C.) maintained in Britain by a number of business institutions to provide expertise to those operating community or social welfare services.

All of these areas ranging from problems of management and management study to the role of dance in a diverse culture, devolution and the function of the private sector, fall within the policy aspect of that area of funding I have called communication. All are to do with policy or, if you like, politics, because it is public attitudes to dance and the thinking of people about dance that we must change before we can hope to get the funds that it and all the arts deserve. The key to this changed thinking, and hence to the future of dance in Canada and its long-term funding, lies in the educational system.

The Arts and Education

The many members of our dance profession who commended my report for the Canada Council about the development of professional training for classical ballet in this country largely ignored its reference to a necessary partnership with public education. Partly this was because of the way the report was presented but also, I think, it is partly because the need for this partnership is somewhat discounted by our profession. It reflects again that isolation to which I have referred. Yet if we seek the development of all kinds of dance in all kinds of places in Canada, as I suggest we should, we cannot achieve our goal in isolation. We must adapt "the forces of geography"; involve institutions like the Banff Centre, York University, Ryerson and others; know what goes on in primary and secondary schools across the country; and be prepared to take a stand on practical matters like the pay, status and conditions of Canadian dance teachers.

So I make no apologies for turning in some detail to education, first on the most practical level of cash resources. If you put together the total sum spent by all levels of government in Canada on education, recreation, leisure and the arts, you will find that education accounts for 93% of this sum, recreation and leisure 6.75% and the arts 0.25%. Even a minute switch in education priorities, and hence in resources, toward the arts would thus make an immense, immediate difference. This is why all dance bodies in search of additional resources should continue urgent dialogue with the world of education around them. At the same time a note is in order to the Canada Council and Federal Government to reconsider established practice. After 25 years, perhaps the time has come to discuss with provincial governments some comprehensive scheme of subvention to assist the arts in education, raising their standards and enlarging their range.

But the main significance of education in funding a bigger future for dance is not short-term cash, but long-term influence. Education, in which I include the educational role of television, provides the biggest single opportunity that a democratic society offers to influence the taxpayer who represents demand on the one hand and subsidy on the other. The level of public subsidy for the arts directly reflects the priorities of our educational system. If over the next 25 years, Canadian schools, teacher training and educational policy were changed to bring the arts nearer the heart of the curriculum, it would benefit the quality of our future as nothing else could do. Therefore it is to this task that many of us in Britain are now giving our attention—seeking to add to the three traditional R's—reading, writing and 'rithmetic—a fourth R, the arts, at the core of British primary and secondary education. In higher education, it is becoming more and more accepted that there are not four great streams of intellectual endeavour—the professions, humanities, sciences and social sciences—but five, adding the creative arts. There is a growing shift in the nature of higher education to reflect this broader view. Today we have, in the United States, Canada, the United Kingdom, Australia and elsewhere, a potentially vast, young, public hooked at school, which apparently sees the arts, especially dance, neither as a dispensable and sinful luxury nor as a holy hobby for superior people, but something to be taken or left as an integral part of living.

The arts and education services would benefit these young people and their future families through a closer working relationship at each level. Young people leaving school would be able to continue their initial exposure to the arts in other ways, through clubs, at their work place, in adult and further education and from provision by arts councils. We need a concentrated attack on cultural inequality, and our schools, universities and arts organizations could lead it. The campuses of the nation, in particular, need to pay more attention to the cultural life of their student communities and the communities around them so that each campus becomes genuinely a cultural centre.

In this sense, then, the long-term future of artists, including dancers, really does lie in the hands of the educators. If our children and grandchildren were offered at all stages of their education the chance of acquiring practice and familiarity, not only with the four R's but with creative action and the habit of discrimination—the chance to make music, poetry, plays, dances, pictures—we would not need to worry about the financial problems of the arts.

Who can persuade the educators? Education and educators, of course, are controlled by provincial and local governments directly influenced by citizens. We need more communication between organs that represent citizens—not just liaison but real communication between arts councils and local government, arts councils and education authorities, arts bodies and broadcasting, arts people, sports people, leisure people. Ultimately, though, it is the citizens who decide, and they will give their support when artists and other enthusiasts learn to present their case effectively, refuse to take no for an answer, organize themselves as pressure groups, acquaint themselves with local government practices, establish a reputation for scrupulous responsibility in using money that is, after all, yours and mine. The drive needs to come from all of us here, even if power lies elsewhere. This is the historic source of progress, be it in housing, child welfare, or education and the arts.

The same source can change attitudes in industry and commerce toward artistic talent. There is a realization slowly spreading among management and unions that the arts are an essential element in work, from the houses we live in to the machines we design, and that the work place is also a place for living. Implicit in this change of attitudes is a concept of the artist, of creative people, as a national resource with something rare to offer, deserving a living wage. After all, it is the consumer, the public, the taxpayer, not the artist, who benefits from funding the arts. The arts educate. The arts inspire and humanize. In a technological society, the arts and education are a partnership essential to the future of each other and of ourselves as human beings.

Conclusion

How, then, do we bring about these changes and apply the lessons of the first 25 years? Above all, through the quality, integrity and artistic and technical excellence of what is offered.

I have suggested a number of ways we might attack the problem of funding across a broad front. The dance world must end its internal rivalries and get itself together. It should embrace the sciences of arts and economics, conduct needed market (i.e. audience) research, draw on professional expertise and conduct surveys, particularly a national survey, to assess and develop the place of the arts in education. A code of sponsorship should be adopted by the business community, unions must be urged to comprehend the arts within their field of activities and each dance company must initiate a regular public education program appropriate to its size and resources. But this is worthless unless the standards are high. Perhaps a "Ballet for All" or "Dance for All" company of the highest professional excellence would help in building audiences and in extending audience appreciation on a national scale.

It seems to me that considerations of this kind are necessary and relevant if the funding of dance and the arts generally is to win the public support it deserves. They are necessary also to answer those funding questions I asked at the beginning—what, which, why, when, where and how? I have not yet answered "who" because the answer falls into two parts. There are those who give and those who do. Both sorts should not fear to think dangerously, live radically and take risks. As Basil Bunting, the English Northumbrian poet once wisely remarked, "A safe new poem is a bad poem."

Beyond this, let me say from experience that the most difficult and haphazard of all the arts is patronage. Art originates with individuals and communicates with individuals. Because of this a successful patron must expect disapproval and endure it. He or she should not fear criticism nor pay too much attention to respectability. The patron must be happy to keep company with young men and women in torn jeans and wild hair who treat authority with contempt and know nothing of bookkeeping. The patron must do without gratitude for it always hampers an artist. To keep such company, in fact, will be the only reward—and for me, as someone who is equally creator, teacher and patron, I want none better. The artist writes no reports, keeps no accounts to be audited (apart from his subsidy), makes no speeches, and thereby makes the world a better place. For if we were *all* artists, the paper work that plagues the administrator would be gone and arts administrators as well as artists would lead happier lives.

Timothy Porteous
Palaces Built on Sand

I do not suppose that many of you have had the opportunity, or the inclination, to read the Canada Council Act, an obscure statute that provides the legal basis for our programs of grants. It contains some surprising provisions. In the list of those forms of art that are considered appropriate for our support, there is no mention of dance. I refer to this regrettable omission not to prove that all Council grants to the National Ballet have been illegal, nor because I am going to ask it to return the $7,275,000 that the Council has provided, in total, since 1957. I raise the point as an illustration of the remarkable progress of dance in this country since the 1950s. At the time the Act was drafted it was not considered necessary to mention dance. Today it is inconceivable that any draftsman, however unfamiliar with the arts in Canada, could leave it out. Undoubtedly the principal agents for this change in awareness have been our three large ballet companies and the manifold activities that have sprung from them or sprung up in reaction to them.

At the Council itself there has been a steady growth in the attention given to dance and in our dance programs. Although the Council approved grants to all three ballet companies in its first year of operation, and has done so in every subsequent year, it was not until 1972 that it set up a separate dance division with its own staff and budget under Monique Michaud.

This year (1976) the dance budget of $3.2 million

will provide operations grants to eight companies and a school, and project grants to another fifteen organizations. (The projected figure for 1978-79 was $3.8 million.) In 1975-76 these grants accounted for almost 25 percent of the budgets of each of the three largest dance companies. Grants from our Touring Office accounted for another 5 percent or so. In the case of the National Ballet, provincial and municipal grants underwrote almost 20 percent of the budget, private fund raising just over 10 percent and the box office, the largest source of revenue, earned just over 50 percent of the total costs.

The question most frequently put to the Council is, "By what formula do you calculate your grants?" Unfortunately, for your peace of mind and ours, we have no magic formula. Given the diversity of the companies we support, I do not believe we could or should have a formula, although in a tight budgetary situation we may have to fall back on an across-the-board minimum rate of growth in our grants. Contrary to widespread belief, we do not accord any special consideration to a Toronto-based company that calls itself "National." Its grant would be no smaller and no larger if it called itself the Royal Toronto Ballet or the Great Canadian Ballet.

In distributing our all-too-finite resources we do take into account (my list is not in order of importance) the size of the previous budget and grant, the quality and costs of the proposed programs, public support as expressed through the box office and private fund raising, the availability of other sources of revenue, management competence, creativity (otherwise known as the Swan Lake Factor) and, most objective of all, artistic excellence. If a

company satisfies all of our requirements we provide
as much money as we can. If not, we provide as little
as we dare. And here I must reveal the most
embarrassing secret of our trade. In a bad year there
may be little or no difference between the two.

So much for the past. What about the future of
funding? Among the questions to which it would be
useful to have answers are: what will funds be needed
for? How much? Where will they come from? Let me
list a few of the demands for additional funds that
will have to be met if we are to have a healthy and
developing dance scene in Canada.

1.)   Survival of existing organizations. As it
seems likely that costs will continue to rise faster than
box office revenues, the income gap of existing
companies will grow even wider. In most countries
dance companies are not expected to pay 50 percent
or even 40 percent of their costs from their box
office, so this problem is not peculiar to Canada.

2.)   Dancers' salaries. Not only are most dancers
underpaid in relation to other occupations requiring
comparable skills and effort, but their employment is
intermittent. They should be regularly employed at
reasonable salaries instead of being part-time wards of
the Unemployment Insurance Commission. We are
about to achieve this status for our orchestra
musicians, so why not for our dancers?

3.)   Choreography. We have to provide more
opportunities for experimental work by
choreographers—probably the most expensive form of
creativity in the performing arts.

4.)   Professional training. In the past almost all
professional training in this country has been
subsidized by some form of commercial teaching.

Rising costs and rising standards make this less and less feasible. Because of constitutional inhibitions this is an area in which federal funding is likely to remain marginal. I commend it to the attention of my colleagues in provincial government, particularly those responsible for education.

    5.)   Dance halls. Many communities are inadequately equipped to present the quality of dance performance which is available and which the public is demanding. At the head of this list I would place Toronto. For some reason capital funds seem easier to raise than operating funds, so we can expect continuing improvement in this area.

    How much will all this cost? The usual technique of futurologists is to measure a past trend and project it on the future. Let us apply this technique to the National Ballet's budget. In 19 years (1957-76) the National Ballet's annual grant from the Canada Council has grown from $50,000 to about $1 million, an average annual growth rate of 17 percent. Assuming this growth rate will moderate slightly to an average of 15 percent over the next 25 years, the Company's grant in the year 2000 will be $32 million. Before getting too enthusiastic about this prospect, we should calculate what it will be costing to run the Company by then. Assuming the 1975-76 budget of $3.4 million will also grow at 15 percent, not an unreasonable expectation based on past experience, the total budget in the year 2000 will be about $112 million. I offer these figures simply to demonstrate the futility of such projections over a long period. Any amount that appears reasonable will be inadequate and any amount that is adequate will appear outrageous.

Nevertheless, I do not think we should be dazzled or discouraged by such statistics. The figures that we accept as normal today would have appeared unbelievable 25 years ago. Many a less prosperous society than ours has been able to devote a much larger proportion of its wealth to the support of the arts. We know that our society has the resources if it wishes to use them for this purpose. Anyone who travels around this country will find evidence of a demand that is growing and that will have to be satisfied.

How rapidly the necessary funds will be made available and from what sources they will come are but two of the uncertainties that underlie the apparent progress of the dance in Canada.

Those of us whose work involves the embodiment of intangible values must learn to live with such uncertainties and even to take defiant pride in them.

When I think of such institutions as the National Ballet and the Canada Council I am reminded of two lines by Edna St. Vincent Millay, with which I will close my remarks.

Safe upon the solid rock the ugly houses stand:
Come and see my shining palace built upon the
sand!

FILM, TELEVISION and VIDEO

Norman Campbell
Margaret Dale

Norman Campbell and Margaret Dale have each made major contributions to the ballet through their work in Canadian and British television respectively.

Although there will continue to be people who resent and oppose the idea that ballet should be performed on either television or film, whether it be in the form of adaptations from the stage or of original choreography, it is clear that in the future the screened media will have an increasing importance for dance.

Here Norman Campbell reflects on his own career as a television and film director, touching upon a number of interesting technical and practical considerations, while Margaret Dale reminds us of a number of important theoretical aspects, offering her own view of how dancers might themselves master the craft of television and film, and summarizing some of the opinions expressed at varous points in the conference.

FILM, TELEVISION and VIDEO

Norman Campbell
A Labour of Love

From time to time, someone—an interviewer, or perhaps a friend—will ask why I have made so many television ballets. I would hope the answer is obvious. I get an enormous kick out of doing it. In fact, I think most television producers, if they were being honest with themselves, would admit that they do shows not primarily for the audience but for themselves, trusting to their instincts and hoping that by following them they may convey their love of something to the people watching at home.

I was lucky in a way because when I first started making television adaptations of classical ballet we broadcast live and as soon as the show was over the phones would start ringing. You soon found out whether people approved. That was in 1956 when we did *Swan Lake* for the first time with the National Ballet of Canada and right then I knew there was an audience for what we had to offer.

Now, everything is taped and may sit on a shelf for months and months before it reaches the screen. But the audience is still there.

Quite clearly, and not just because of my professional involvement, I am convinced that television has an important function to play in bringing some of the magic of ballet to people who might otherwise never see it. On the one hand, in a country as vast as Canada, we can reach out to audiences who are too far removed from the big cities to see our large touring companies live, on stage. Then again, we have convincing evidence that many of our viewers who have seen productions of the big classics on television are curious enough to want to see the live version.

I think the National Ballet would freely admit that the CBC production of *Romeo and Juliet* that we presented in 1965 had a positive impact on their box office. In my own terms it may be the most important ballet production I have done.

Somehow the fact that we were still working in black and white did not seem to matter. It suited the Mediterranean setting of the story and the classic beauty of our then teen-aged star, Veronica Tennant.

However, I do not want to give the impression that television exists simply as an extension of the stage and as a means for publicizing what goes on there. When a ballet moves to television it has to change and, ironically, must do so if it is to remain true to its original conception.

At the moment we seem to be going through a phase of "live from" presentations where, essentially, the camera places itself in the theatre and broadcasts what happens on stage. Sometimes it works, but too often the producer finds himself in the same position as his colleague trying to televise a sports event. Apart from lighting problems that can leave great, gaping black spaces on the viewer's screen, you are presented with groups of people spread out in patterns that do not ideally suit the television medium.

From my point of view, the "live from" approach runs the risk of turning the clock back to straight theatre, ignoring the enormous technical possibilities of television—and, for that matter, of film. Although we were fortunate enough to win an Emmy award in 1973 for our production of Rudolf Nureyev's *The Sleeping Beauty*, which was recorded, live to tape, at the O'Keefe Centre in Toronto, that experience was not as rewarding for me, nor I believe as effective for the viewing audience, as what we can achieve in a studio taping situation. In the case of *The Sleeping Beauty*, it was a shoot first, ask questions later approach. We had six recording machines running continuously, one for each camera, churning out miles and miles of tape and we were left with an incredible editing job afterward.

My own preference is for a more controlled and carefully planned taping where, in effect, we have done a certain amount of pre-editing in the rehearsal hall.

In most cases, my guide and inspiration is the music. Perhaps the greatest joy I get from producing ballet for television is to move cameras to music without having to think about dialogue. It's like a great breath of pure, fresh air in an otherwise cacophonous world—just letting the music flow over us like water.

So, my approach in the planning stages, having

familiarized myself with the plot and choreography, is to mark up a working score of the music. As rehearsals progress, camera angles and movements are written into the score with the moment for a switch from one camera to another marked right on the beat. Of course, when it comes to actual taping, we may decide to hold a shot for just a hair, or take it just a fraction earlier. Those are matters of judgment and ultimately it depends on the sensitivity of the man who is physically in control of the switch. But the point is that we have already got a general plan. It allows us to tape quite lengthy segments at one go.

In film, it is different. For a variety of technical reasons, shooting tends to proceed much more slowly. A scene is set up, the lighting is adjusted. The dancers ready themselves and then, if you are lucky, you will do 30 seconds or so before another shot has to be prepared. Meanwhile, the dancers are getting cold, or tired, or both. I've worked a good deal in film and I know how gruelling it can be for everyone. There's no question that dancers have an easier time in the television studio.

The technical characteristics of the film medium and the traditional camera work of film people tend to make them see dance movement laterally. In television, the most effective movement is the other way, in and out, from back to front, in long, tunnel-like shots. That's why things such as big, wide crowd scenes can present real difficulties for television. However, the problems are more easily resolved in a studio than on stage during a performance.

It's not a question of changing actual steps. That is rarely done. However, groupings may be realigned and the spacing is adjusted to conform with the technical needs of television.

Naturally, as soon as you start doing that sort of thing someone among the dancers or direction of a company is going to start worrying. The only way you can dispel their uncertainty is to show them what can be achieved. There has to be confidence between the television producer/director and the artistic staff of the company with whom you are working. If the choreographer is a living one, his trust also has to be won.

During my long working association with the National Ballet I think we have established that trust. Sometimes you have to prove a point. When we came to propose a television production of Erik Bruhn's version of *Swan Lake* I showed him *Romeo and Juliet*. The necessary trust was established and the production went ahead. But somewhere along the way, it has to be clear who is boss. Someone has to be responsible for certain decisions in making a television ballet and ultimately that should be the television director.

It comes down to a matter of taste—of good taste. If the people you are working with accept that you respect the material and intend to treat it with integrity then all will be well. Sometimes that is not easy for them. There will always be those who feel that what I like to call the "magic" of television, the electronic and optical effects that can be achieved, should not be used in a production of classical ballet. Yet it is hard to envisage the production we did of Célia Franca's *Cinderella* in 1968 without those special effects. They enhanced the fantasy of the story and actually gave the ballet an extra dimension it could not have had on stage. It also won us an Emmy in 1970.

The television director's responsibility is a considerable one. He is making visual decisions that his audience must either accept or reject. It takes us back to that miraculous device we carry around with us and through which we perceive the outside world. The human eye, together with the mind, is continually seeing shots. There may not be an actual frame, but the "mind's eye" mentally obliterates what it does not want to see.

As you know, a good choreographer, like a good drama director, can to some extent control the attention of an audience member, especially in story ballets. However, the television director has to make continuous decisions where ordinarily the audience in a theatre has some degree of choice. Will it be a wide shot, capturing the full spectacle of a passage of corps work? Will it be a close-up that captures the expression on one dancer's face? All the time, one is, in effect, trying to put the television audience in the best seat, wherever that might be, for each moment of a ballet. And then, because the television image is contained within a frame, you have to make sure the odd hand or foot does not get cut out of the picture. That can present real difficulties if you are shooting a jump in a studio that is not high enough and if, in the actual taping, the dancer soars higher than you had anticipated.

One of the most frequent criticisms levelled against television ballet is that there is not enough space around the dancers: too many two-shots and three-shots (that is, two or three people in the frame) in isolation from the scene as a whole.

One way around that is to have the camera pull back to give the feeling of air around the dancers so you can see them move through space, rather than move with them. Sometimes, it works to have the camera move in a complementary direction. There might be a great revolving pattern in the choreography and you move the camera around it either in the same direction or opposite. It can give a marvellously dramatic sense of movement.

As you have probably gathered, I am very much for moving cameras about and I rather regret the fact that when we are kind to the dancers' bodies and build them a nice wooden floor in the studio, it is at a cost of camera mobility because the cameras today are still heavy machines and most constructed studio stages are not stable enough to support them: they have to stay on the concrete floor.

Not long ago, an interviewer asked me how much I'd been helped over the years by advancing technology and when I thought about it I had to say that the changes and developments were not that significant.

Of course, the introduction of colour to CBC-TV in 1967 enormously enhanced the quality and effect of televised ballet, as it did most programs. Then there was the introduction, with the new colour cameras, of zoom lenses on all our machines—and I'm not sure how much of a benefit that was.

The zoom lens has the capacity to change its focal length, and therefore its angle of vision, continuously, over a particular range, without going out of focus. Before the zoom, one had a set of lenses of varying focal lengths and you "racked" over from one to another—or you actually moved the camera in or out, toward or away from the subject. All one has to do now is press a button and, optically, you have pulled yourself in close to the subject. The effect in terms of television image is, however, quite different from that achieved by moving the camera and I think it's generally inferior. A kind of laziness has crept in with zoom lenses. I like to move the camera, as I have said, with the music, and that to me makes for more exciting television.

There seems to me to be a number of technological developments that should occur though, unfortunately, it is going to take a revolution, in all probability, to make them happen.

Our cameras have already become lighter and smaller than they were when I began 25 years ago. However, we need to exploit the technology of modern micro-circuitry much more to give us even lighter equipment that will enable us to move steadily over almost any surface. That much is within easy reach.

More fundamental is the need to do something about the quality of the television image. We have to get away from our 525 line system to produce images with greater resolution of detail that can be enlarged to deliver the kind of impact we get from film. Looking at Herbert Ross's *The Turning Point*, I could not help but envy the beauty and quality of what he could achieve on film. I know we now have devices that can project and enlarge the television image onto a screen but the picture is still made up of those 525 lines; only instead of looking like string the lines are blown up to look like rope. Somehow we have to achieve the quality of film in television.

There is another point about future developments about which I feel very strongly and it is not a technical matter. It has to do with the availability of the programs we have already made. Generally, because of financial restraints, a broadcasting organization pays the performers for one or perhaps two showings. After that the show is effectively lost. Unless someone happened to pirate it off the air, students of dance and those in isolated communities far removed from the touring circuits, are denied the opportunity to see our major Canadian companies in full productions—orchestra, costumes—the full spectacle.

Technically, the process of transferring from video to 16mm film is simple. The problem arises over performers' contracts. Someone has to pay the step-up fees to revise those contracts so that films of television productions can be made available to schools, research centres and to community organizations. I do not think the broadcasting organizations themselves are going to be able to find the money.

I see it as a marvellous opportunity for big corporations and foundations to make a major contribution to our cultural life. All they have to do is send money and in return they will have good exposure as the sponsor of films that will go right across Canada. We have a visual archive just sitting there doing nothing at present. Something needs to be done about it.

I have been talking from a very personal viewpoint on the basis of my own experience as a television producer working primarily with large companies in adapting major classical ballet for the small screen. There are, of course, many other aspects to the general subject of television and ballet. What I think is undeniable is the fact that television has become a major factor in the presentation of dance. It is not going to substitute for live stage performance but will continue, within its limitations—which, I hope, will become fewer and fewer—to bring the magic of ballet to a vast audience. For me, working with ballet has provided the most exciting moments of my career. I am very grateful for them.

Margaret Dale
A Broader Vision

I think film, television and video have a special significance for dance and this significance is important for those of us within the dance community, as well as for those who write about it, and for those who study dance or who choreograph. As Selma Landen Odom wrote in the Art Gallery of Ontario's publication *Dance and Film* (1977), "they have brought new possibilities for seeing and making dance."

One of the problems encountered in talking about film, television and video in relation to dance arises from the fact that we tend to use the words in several different senses. For instance, when we use the term "film," we can be referring to the medium of film, as, for example, in the statement: "Film preceded television." Or we may be referring to a particular film: "It was a good film." Or perhaps we mean the physical substance: "The film was scratched."

Similarly with the word "television," we can be

referring to the medium—television is a powerful communications medium—or to the signal. Unlike film, television has no substance: it is a signal, a telecommunications device. But usually, when we mention television, we are referring to the programs provided by broadcasting organizations; we really mean broadcast television.

It is the same with "video," a 20th century word that came into general use in the 1960s, after it became possible to record a TV picture onto magnetic tape. "Video" can mean a variety of different things.

I have always been intrigued by the two-way relationship that exists between the worlds of film, television and video, and the world of dance.

As I see it, dance can serve the world of film as it does in the case of Herbert Ross's *The Turning Point*, where dance is the subject of "a movie." Movies are produced by businessmen for the film industry. Movies aim to be popular entertainment for a mass audience. Their appeal is to the emotions. Now, what is really happening when a film producer makes a movie with a story set in the world of dance is that he is responding to a recognizable public interest. It means that he has decided that the subject of dance is sufficiently popular with a large enough group of people to justify the expense of making the movie. It does not mean that he cares about building the audience for dance into one that is both knowledgeable and critical. The opposite relationship—the one where film serves the world of dance—is the one that interests me most. Film as a medium is superior to words when describing movement. Film is a great medium for the individual wishing to explore and illuminate an aspect of dance, a great medium for writing about dance, and a good medium for learning about it.

A similar two-way relationship exists between the worlds of television and of dance. Recently, dance served television when WNET in New York mounted its *Dance in America* series. The series was made by a broadcasting organization as part of its general television programming. Again, once an audience interest emerges, TV will popularize it. Equally, as viewers' attitudes change when, for instance, a passing interest in ballet seems to be superceded by a vogue for Olympic gymnastics, so the TV programs disappear.

It is the other relationship—the one where the tools and techniques of television serve dance—that intrigues me. I look forward to the day when dance scholars will be publishing on video-tape. I want dance films made by dance people that will belong to the dance profession. I want to see a dance-film library. I believe that film, television and video are essential to our growth and development and that they can advance the world of dance.

The National Ballet of Canada's conference did not attempt to focus on these 20th century inventions or their interchanges and relationships with dance. Nor were the "new possibilities" explored by key speakers or specialist panels.

This conference was primarily a celebration, a 25th anniversary. What it did was to address themes: music, design, choreography, funding, criticism, and so on, that revealed the preoccupations of a ballet company coping with the realities of artistic and economic survival in the late 20th century.

I suspect that the National Ballet's conference

organizers knew that illuminating discussion on such complex subjects really required a forum of its own—a conference to itself. Nevertheless, Vincent Tovell, in his capacity as chairman, skilfully guided the discussions, allowing the topics of film, television and video to come up in a very spontaneous way.

In fact, film and television were represented by screenings: two televised ballets, Martha Graham's *Appalachian Spring* (WQED, 1958) and *Giselle* (CBC-TV, 1976); one filmed ballet, Frederick Ashton's *Enigma Variations,* directed by James Archibald, (1969); and a documentary film, *The Making of a Ballet* (1969), commissioned by the Dutch government, about Rudi van Dantzig's *Painted Birds.*

These were evening viewings and they were really doing duty for live performance. They were not shown to underline, illustrate, or emphasize any major ideas that had arisen during the day. They were simply there as entertainment, as something to see after a long day's talk.

It would be misleading though to give the impression that no interesting or provocative ideas were voiced in any of the talk sessions. On the contrary, several times there were direct and indirect references to the interchanges of film, television and video with dance. You could say they amounted to a kind of sub-text to the major topics of discussion.

What I have tried to do here is to assemble some of the views that emerged through the conference, with the hope of placing them in some sort of context. The quoted extracts that follow have been grouped, for the sake of this article, under appropriate headings.

The Relation of Ballet Companies to Broadcasting Organizations

Television does have an enormous value (for all ballet companies) in preparing a very, very large audience for ballet.

Alexander Grant

Too many of the media's decision-makers (in Canada) are clinging to the outdated prejudices that have greatly hampered ballet's image in this country.

Veronica Tennant

We must express gratitude to television. We owe very much to Pierre Mercure; our company was actually born from his TV show (L'heure du concert).

Ludmilla Chiriaeff

More and more, I think, (ballet) companies will televise themselves. They will free themselves from CBC-TV, BBC-TV, and all those (broadcasting) organizations and they will do it themselves.

Margaret Dale

Television as a Medium for the Performance of Ballet, A Theatre Art

I'm awaiting the day when it will be three-dimensional, and until it is, it is no good to the ballet really.

Dame Ninette de Valois

It is a different medium. As Marshall McLuhan said, "The medium is the message." It is a great mistake to expect to have the same experience....

Margaret Dale

I would always prefer to perform on stage.
Veronica Tennant

The Role of Film and Video in Dance Education

Dance was man's earliest form of communication, but until these new developments it has not been possible to study it. Suddenly we can write our own history—and in visual terms. What we need is a visual literature. Every dancer can work on this, and do it.... They must learn to use these tools and write their own history.

Margaret Dale

Career Possibilities

There are so many things in the world for ballet dancers to do when they have finished dancing.
Alexander Grant

Margaret Dale suggested earlier that they all come and work for the CBC.
Vincent Tovell

Well, no. I didn't mean it quite like that. I thought they might learn how to use cameras and audiovisual aids as tools and then go their own way, not necessarily the CBC way or any television company's way.

I think that dancers must become their own videographers, and choreographers, and their own recordists: film (and video) recording will complement notation. One day we will have a visually literate generation of dancers who will control their own destinies.

CHOREOGRAPHY

Robert Joffrey

Rudi van Dantzig   *Brian Macdonald*

Choreography is the art (and craft) of making dances. If someone says to a choreographer, "What do you do?", he will most probably answer, "Come and see!" Choreography is not something easily talked about.

Not surprisingly, therefore, the internationally distinguished contributors to this section do not attempt to discuss the artistic process of making ballets so much as to comment on the external conditions that affect their creation.

Once again there is plentiful reference to history and tradition. As Sir Frederick Ashton suggests in his foreword, those who try to ignore tradition are simply being unrealistic.

CHOREOGRAPHY

Robert Joffrey
Past and Present: The Vital Connection

For the choreographer, the last part of the 20th century is a wonderful and exciting age to live in. Great possibilities lie ahead although, as I shall explain later, there are certain dangers we must avoid. Our best course is to recognize fully the nature of the revolution that has taken place in dance during this century. A promising future has been laid before us, but first we must take stock of our inheritance.

We begin with Fokine. He brought a new expressiveness to ballet which, when one remembers that *Raymonda* was still quite new, can only be called revolutionary. While the classical ballet was still preoccupied with the technique of steps, Fokine created *The Dying Swan* (1905) for Anna Pavlova in which the steps, mainly *bourrées*, were subordinated to the spirit of the dance as a whole. What was important was the *quality* of the movement in which

Fokine fulfilled a set of principles he had already established for the choreographer.

For Fokine, dance must be expressive, not mere gymnastics, reflecting true feeling of character, appropriately set in time and space. Gesture and mime must not be mechanical and conventional but should suit the style of each ballet. Similarly, the costumes must be consistent with the ballet's plot, not just the established conventional classical styles. Above all, in Fokine's mind, the ballet should be more than a series of separate steps and variations. It should possess a flow of movement giving it a unity that must not be broken by an audience applauding particular virtuoso "numbers." These are still very important ideas.

When one remembers that *Les Sylphides* came only a decade after *Raymonda*, the importance of the change introduced by Fokine is apparent. There, in *Les Sylphides*, there are no steps to attract applause; it is the flow, the musicality, the quality of movement that is paramount.

Fokine gave us a new freedom. Once, in Russia, he wanted the dancers in a new ballet to be barefooted. The theatre would not allow this. So, he had the dancers paint toe-nails on their tights, put rouge on their knees—and all this before Isadora Duncan made an impression. Think of *Petrouchka*, the way Fokine utilized the folk dance of his own country; not Russian peasant dances as they would have been danced in the streets, of course, but the essence of the movements characterized for the theatre. Think of the costumes: hardly a tutu, only for The Ballerina, and very little work on point. In *Schéhérazade* no one is on point. It was not too popular with the dancers at the start. Most dancers wanted to be in tutus and on point, just as the audience expected to see them. But Fokine persisted, leaving us such a heritage. It was a complex process, achieving the unity of elements that Fokine desired in a ballet. It makes it hard to revive his ballets, now that he is no longer with us to supervise their rehearsal.

We know from students and from what Fokine himself said that he felt he needed his own specially trained dancers. Only the choreographer himself can give *quality* to his steps. It cannot be done at the barre. That was his lesson to us. To Fokine the creative part of a class was found only in centre work.

Balanchine took us ahead a stage further with his new perception of the relationship between music and dance. In writing about Stravinsky's music for *Agon*, Balanchine in fact set out new choreographic guidelines. Music, in his view, cannot be *illustrated* by dance. The movement must be a visual equivalent, a complement rather than an illustration. Stravinsky was a subtle organizer of rhythm and Balanchine was inspired by the way in which each measure of the composer's music had its own personal style. It was a living unit in which even the empty spaces between sounds are not void. "Life goes on within each silence."

Here one finds a very different concept of the choreographer. One senses the great admiration, the deep respect that Balanchine has for Stravinsky. Theatrically, *Agon* is miles apart from *Petrouchka* and *Spectre de la rose* but possesses its own special qualities, the individuality of the creator. One realizes the importance of vitality, energy, rhythm, the use of space, all qualities Mr. Balanchine brings to his ballets. One sees how concerned he is with the execution of the movement and its relation to the music. And just as we have observed that there were Fokine dancers, so we have Balanchine dancers, trained specially to suit his choreography in the school he created. He demands unique qualities in dancers. For him these are of consuming importance.

No one should be surprised if I now mention Martha Graham. How fortunate we are to have her as part of our age. It is not too much to say that she created a whole new way of moving; the contractions, the falls—they have become part of our dance vocabulary. But it is not only movement.

Her sense of theatre, her lighting, her use of props, her use of the stage itself, has been an inspiration to countless choreographers.

Perhaps one does not think of Frederick Ashton as a rebel, as one easily does of Fokine, Balanchine and Graham. Yet, in a sense, apart from the marvellous lyrical flow of his choreography, Ashton has helped to revolutionize the modern pas de deux. In Ashton we do not see one person just carrying somebody else across the stage. We see a relationship of man and woman, a combination of movement that goes beyond partnership. It is choreography with invention and, most importantly, artistic motivation.

It is a curious thing. In the 1930s it was assumed that the ballet had to be Russian. If you were English or American you changed your name to fit into the ballet world. As Hurok, the impresario, used to say, "Only Russians can dance." I remember when Ballet Theatre began it was always, "The Best in Russian Ballet"—and this was *American* Ballet Theatre!

Now, two of the earliest choreographers to work with the Ballet Russe de Monte Carlo were Frederick

Ashton, an Englishman, who in 1939 created *Devil's Holiday* and Marcel Le Plat, an American boy, who created *Ghost Town* under the name Marc Platoff. Incidentally, the music for *Ghost Town* was by an interesting young composer called Richard Rodgers.

Neither of these ballets has survived, but they marked a breakthrough, just as did Ninette de Valois' departure from the Diaghilev company. The very idea of founding a British ballet company! I am sure her fellow dancers never thought she would succeed.

If one were to poll today's choreographers I think you would find a majority are English-speaking. How far we have come from the twenties and thirties.

I have spoken of rebels, of pathmakers and pioneers, but of course we must not forget our heritage in the classics, even if they have not passed down to our day in their original form. That may be just as well. Perhaps it is what has kept them alive. We know that *Giselle* was not all danced on point. Yvette Chauviré, the French ballerina, was careful to dance many of the steps in *Giselle* on half point. We know that in some cases what today is accepted as Bournonville style could not have been danced in the shoes that existed in his era.

What has happened is that little changes have been made by successive ballet masters. In a way the classics have been updated to keep abreast of technical developments in the ballet.

But what of today's choreographer, the beneficiary of such a rich heritage with so many avenues open before him? What must he do with his freedom, which today will even allow him to have dancers stand absolutely still on stage, simply because it is what he wants?

It is a freedom we expect to be used responsibly and with respect. If it works for the artistic idea behind the ballet, then it is right. We are looking for a clear, individual expression, for the sense that nobody but that one choreographer could quite do that ballet to that piece of music in quite that way.

In achieving this, the choreographer has to maintain the trust of the dancers, especially when he is doing something in a way that is new. When he goes into that studio and faces however many dancers it is for the first time, he must sweep away their anxiety and insecurity. Dancers worry a good deal. What kind of movement is he going to give me? Will I get a solo? Can I look good in it? The choreographer certainly has to have full command of his medium, and that means knowing all he can about theatre: costumes, lighting, decor, music. Most of all, he must know how to draw the best from the dancers. That means convincing them that the movement he gives them is the right movement for them. He must help them translate it through their own bodies. They have to be able to add something. Once the curtain goes up, it is theirs—theirs to make live.

It is a tremendous responsibility for the choreographer and for the director of a company who must take into his care the handling of a ballet once the choreographer has finished working with it. In a company with a large and varied repertoire, that entails maintaining the distinctions in style between one choreographer's work and another while recognizing that your company will not perform, say, a Balanchine ballet in the way his own company does. I may say here, that I believe strongly in giving as many people as possible the opportunity to see great ballets. At a time when touring has become difficult because of the costs involved that means an end to exclusive performing rights for particular companies.

For the future, directors have another responsibility, to make it easier for choreographers to work. The pressures today have become impossible. We expect choreographers to work quickly, to create a ballet in perhaps four weeks. We would not expect the composer of a new score to do that although he has, like a painter or writer, the great luxury of working quietly at home. He can put his work away without anyone seeing. He even has the chance to rework it.

How many times the poor choreographer would like to pause. But no, it is scheduled for December 12 at 8 o'clock. It must be ready. And if it is not an immediate success it hardly lasts the season and it is a long time before that choreographer is asked again.

It has become so costly now. The choreographer needs studio space, dancers, music. There has to be a way to allow young choreographers a chance to experiment, to take risks, to fail without jeopardizing a career.

Perhaps we should return to Balanchine for a moment. One forgets how many ballets he created for opera. This is a wonderful place for a choreographer to start. You still have time to work, even more so since the dance is not the principal element, but you get valuable experience under less critical scrutiny. After all, people come to opera for the music and singing and your little five minutes of dance may not be mentioned at all in the review. But then again, it might be.

Choreography is a craft as well as an art. The

opera demands craftsmanship from a choreographer,
the ability to work in a prescribed style—and to a set
length. I am sometimes a little alarmed by some of
our young choreographers who do not respect that
element of craftsmanship. They have decided to
create. Very well. But were they really experienced
dancers first? Do they know how not to abuse
dancers' bodies? Do they know enough about their
dance heritage to create? These are things they must
have. Think what a tremendous background
Balanchine and Ashton had.

I have looked back and forward. The next 25
years must provide answers to the problems
confronting a new generation of choreographers. We
must help them. They must help themselves too. The
way was opened up for them during the earlier part of
this century. Now the rest lies before them.

Rudi van Dantzig

A Question of Values

I am not the first in this conference either to look into
the past before speculating about the future or to pay
tribute to the great tradition from which we all stem.
However, I will not apologize for doing both these
things since they are so important.

We have heard much of Diaghilev and of the
wonderfully creative era he helped to bring about. Let
us remember, however, that when he wanted
something new for his repertoire he turned *back* to
The Sleeping Beauty. He would never let go of the

classical tradition. Nor must we in the coming 25 years.

We still have among us dancers and choreographers from that era. We must learn from them. Those who grew from the great Russian tradition understand what expressiveness is in dance. Dance truly was a language. The body spoke through a pas de bourrée, an arabesque, an attitude. We must use our modern technology, film, video—anything that will serve to keep this heritage before us. It is in great danger of being lost.

Diaghilev displayed art through great dancers from a great school. The future will depend on the quality of our schools. They are vitally important. Balzac once wrote that only one feeling in youth can rival love and that is love for art. This love for art must begin in the schools—and not just ballet schools. We must help children to perceive beauty, to keep their mind and whole personality open, honest and receptive. Sometimes I fear we close children's minds.

There has been talk of fund-raising. I acknowledge its importance but I also have some worries about it. I worry about our whole materialistic society, our endless demands, our waste of resources that cannot be replaced. It is a grim future and I wonder, after another 25 years, if there will be anything left for the generation after that.

The concept of stardom has introduced another danger—"superstars" asking huge sums to perform. It is unhealthy and unfair. I feel similarly about unions, especially in Canada and the United States. They pose a great threat to the progress of art in general. People's demands finally become impossible. They will destroy themselves. I heard about a choreographer involved with our own company who said he could not create a ballet unless paid a certain amount. It made me very sad.

What a choreographer needs is a body and, maybe, a studio. After the last war we were visited in Holland by fantastic ballet companies from England, America, even from Russia, which had emerged or struggled through very hard times. There was little food, little time to train. Now I always seem to hear dancers complain. I do not want to sound like one of those boring people who always claim how different it was in their youth but I see a danger. We should accept less if need be. Our priority is dance, not money.

As a choreographer today, I feel the need to be aware of the world and what goes on in it. We live in an age of political corruption, of taking, not giving. This is the world our dancers live in.

Let me say a little about ballet in Holland. Although we lack a school and our own tradition we have always had a very serious approach to dance. Maybe it is not a virtuoso approach, perhaps it is a dark view of dance. We do not see dance as amusement. Dance has its own identity.

On our North American tour we presented a repertoire where there were no flowers, no crowns, no tutus, no Minkus music. Dance hardly needs flowers. It should be pure, simple, clear. It definitely does not need crowns.

For the young choreographers there must be resolution: resolution for the audience and the creator. It is a problem with choreography. If a work is found to be too progressive for audiences to immediately understand it is dropped and lost. Yet later audiences might have approved.

It is different in other arts. From Bach to Mozart was a great leap. From Mozart to Beethoven must have been a bigger step and from Tchaikovsky, via Rimsky-Korsakov, to Stravinsky was even a great shock and revolution. A similar argument could be drawn from painting. But painting and music are written down on canvas and paper. The work of choreographers, even with the development of notation, is more vulnerable. It tends to be written down only if it is an immediate success. So much is lost.

However, I retain my faith. New geniuses will come, new Picassos, new Stravinskys, new Balanchines and new Ashtons. They well not even need a Diaghilev. If necessary they will show themselves. But the future they must move into is clouded, full of uncertainty. Life is a variation on the theme of an enigma.

Brian Macdonald

The Chance to Dream

To a man who has been choreographing now for over 20 years, it still remains a mysterious process that I do not really understand very well myself. I do not know why I choose a particular piece of music, I do not know where the courage comes from to stand up in front of dancers and say, "Now dear, you come from that corner on that foot and you do this." I do not know why I choose the collaborators I do except that there are some kinds of vibrations that induce me to think I will work well with them. I don't know why I move from one style to another. I recently looked back on four works I had done in five years and discovered that a particular chain of movement had gone through all the ballets. I had become very absorbed with people holding hands and all the permutations and combinations of the way dancers could revolve around each other without letting go. What prompted that to happen at that stage in my career, I have no idea. Why did I do two comedies in a row? I have no idea.

Choreography is more than a mysterious process. It is often terrifying. You are in terror because you are not quite sure where it is all coming from; it might dry up. You are in terror because you are at the mercy of unions, of economic factors, of deadlines, of sometimes tired dancers or uncooperative dancers, or you have to extend yourself so far to help them come on to your wavelength. You are terrified by what the newspapers might say or whether you are going to have to go into overtime at the dress rehearsal, or whether you should have cancelled the ballet until next year so you can work on it a little longer. If a ballet is very successful, your terror is of what might happen if you change the cast. You are eaten alive by doubts but somehow there is a monkey on your back and you keep going. Over the years you produce a body of work and, if you are lucky enough that some of it survives, you can look back on it and begin to deduce something about the creative spirit.

Choreography is an extraordinarily lonely profession. I have searched nearly all of my professional life for an artistic director to work with, someone who would not only hold my hand in the back of the theatre at the dress rehearsal, but collaborate with me when I am choosing a composer, a conductor even, when I am looking at costume sketches, or making schedules. Somehow the choreographer today has become a loner. He has become responsible for his own work to an almost destructive extent.

When I began, I did college shows, fashion shows, aquatic shows and ice shows; anything I could do to move bodies around. I was a young music critic when Celia Franca arrived in 1950. I thought, this is going to be glorious, here I am a young fellow with a head full of ideas and here is this woman with all her energy and background. She has already indicated a great deal of strength and she is going to make a company. How marvellous. Well, I gather I am rather a prickly fellow, as that didn't work out as I hoped it might. Then I started to work with Arnold Spohr and the Royal Winnipeg Ballet. He was learning as I was learning. You might say we propped each other up for a few years while his company grew and I learned my profession and he learned his.

Sometime later, in 1962, I had a phone call out of a clear blue sky from Mr. Joffrey. Una Kai had seen a videotape of one of my ballets in Winnipeg. "Why don't you come and do something for me?" Joffrey said. Now what an incredible gamble that was! I do not believe he really knew my last name. Somebody had seen something with merit and he took a chance. That is a point I will return to. I remember it all very vividly. I worked with an artistic director. I chose two pieces of music and we phoned the composer and asked him if we could put them together—they had been written 30 years apart. I did the ballet, *Time Out of Mind*, in three weeks under

very difficult circumstances with very good dancers.
He gave me excellent advice about the dancers. This
one will help you, that one won't, this one is busy, try
that one, this one has another quality. Then when the
ballet was finished, he sat back and said, "I don't like
that passage." Well, I could have killed him! I was so
passionately involved with the piece. But a little
something whispered, "That man's right." So I
changed it. Then we were going to take the ballet to
Russia, its premiere was to have been at the
Maryinsky in Leningrad. We were desperately rushed,
working in a rotten little New York theatre going
through dress rehearsals. Bob sat there as though no
union in the world mattered. We could go overtime
until three o'clock in the morning, but we were going
to get that lighting cue right and he did not like this
costume. I was cared for. I was protected. I have
never forgotten it and I think probably I have been
searching for that continuously in my professional
career and have turned very much to my collaborators
for the kind of counsel that should ideally come from
an artistic director. I have never found it in one
person, but I have found in various collaborators
enough strength to help me time and again.

Somewhere in the next 25 years, choreographers
have to be helped by artistic directors who absorb the
pressures, who make the schedules, who keep the
money problems from us, who abet our dreams and
make us extend ourselves. Many years ago in Holland
I was working for the first time with the Het
Nationale Ballet, the company that Rudi van Dantzig
now runs. It was then under the direction of Sonia
Gaskell, another prickly person. She had created the
company after the war and held it in a very firm grip

while she developed it. Something had not gone very well and I had raised my voice in an office somewhere and she had calmed me down and she said, "You looked at Rudi's rehearsal yesterday did you?... What do you think?" I told her. She said, "Well, you know, I try to protect him. I just want him to get up in the morning and dream until his first rehearsal. If he wants he can lie in bed and dream, do whatever he wants. I just want him to dream." We don't have enough of that in ballet companies today.

I should perhaps end by dealing with my own identity as a choreographer. I am a Canadian. To an extent, it is apparent in my work. Yet it is a difficult thing to analyze what exactly a Canadian choreographer is. He is obviously not a man who does a ballet about an Indian legend. He does not always work to a Canadian composer. What makes his work neither English nor American? Where is the aesthetic formed by which, when you walk into the theatre, you look and say, that is the work of *my* country, of this part of the world. The way we move, our musicality, our values on the stage, the subject we choose to dance about, the way we carve up space is peculiar to Canada and it is peculiar to me for reasons I cannot yet define. This morning, I had a very sad thought. Perhaps it is not the way to leave you, but let me explain it anyway. Ballet is incredibly international. A director can pick up a phone, call in a choreographer, pick what he is certain will be a success by shopping in the international supermarket. I do not want to be a chauvinist, well, maybe I do, but I find this a sad state of affairs in Canada. The combined budgets of the Royal Winnipeg Ballet, Les Grands Ballets Canadiens and the National Ballet of

Canada total well over $7 million. I doubt very much whether we are spending more than $10,000 on new music by Canadian composers. I have a strange feeling that my company could go on very well for five years on the repertoire it has at the moment. The National Ballet does not really need the new work of Canadian choreographers or Canadian composers. The Royal Winnipeg Ballet could survive very well by occasionally taking part of its grant and buying a safe ballet. So here we have created three fine companies that can exist without the Canadian choreographer or the Canadian composer. In the next 25 years we should perhaps all consider that as our foremost problem.

At the time of the conference, all three main speakers were company directors as well as choreographers. Together they introduced a very broad range of topics, only a few of which were able to be discussed.

Rudi van Dantzig's passionate concern for social, political and economic problems in the future, his anxiety that dancers might become distracted by too great a concern for material comfort, drew warm response from many listeners. Dame Ninette de Valois, in particular, reminded the audience that the artist enjoyed an essentially privileged position in society for which he must be thankful. She then elaborated on the matter of Diaghilev's restaging of *The Sleeping Beauty*, mentioned by Mr. van Dantzig in his address.

"Many people said Diaghilev revived *Sleeping Beauty* because he was in a jam. He was then between two choreographers: Nijinsky going, Massine gone and Fokine—well, they hadn't spoken to each other for years. Balanchine was still quite young. Perhaps he was in a jam, but one must remember that Diaghilev adored the classical ballet and although people said he was acting ten years too soon, the production was like a shot in the arm for the company. As we all know, he lost money but then rearranged the first and last acts. *Aurora's Wedding*, by the way, known in the company as "Aurora's Bedding," was toured for many years. Europe had not seen pure classical dancing for some time. It was a big draw. Diaghilev had not made a mistake.

"I know it was the only ballet we were all frightened of. It was so exacting technically and sent shivers through the company for days before a performance. Actually, I had just come from Cecchetti and could not understand why they were all so nervous. It seemed they tried to give me every bit of quick dancing there was to do. In a sense I was a good bit ahead of some of the real ballerinas in technique. However, I'm not comparing myself with Nemchinova or Danilova. Which brings me to a subject of great concern in choreography today. The canvas has got to be much broader than it was before, but please remember that there is a distinction between the pure classical dancer and the contemporary dancer. Talented choreographers of today are perfectly capable of understanding this. I beg them to recognize the different requirements in physique and temperament.

"In an orchestra you don't say to the first violin, just as he's going on, 'Oh, by the way, double bassoon tonight if you please.' Nor would you ask the real soprano to sing contralto.

"However, there is a middle-ground occupied by the demi-caractère dancer. It is worth remembering in casting a ballet and holds wonderful possibilities for today's choreographers."

The subject of music was reintroduced by the National Ballet's principal conductor, George Crum, who wanted to know how the panelists felt about working with a new score.

All the choreographers emphasized how important it is for the choreographer and the composer to share a similar artistic and aesthetic viewpoint. They must have a trusting relationship.

There are however many practical problems connected with the rehearsal of a ballet to new music. Brian Macdonald, who has collaborated on five ballets with Canadian composer Harry Freedman, explained the various subterfuges he has resorted to in order to get a tape of the orchestral version of a score. As Robert Joffrey explained, in the case of modern music especially, it is important for dancers to become accustomed to hearing which instruments carry the theme. The piano score alone can be misleading in rehearsal.

Mr. Macdonald suggested arranging an early orchestra rehearsal and sneaking a recording then. It is so hard to choreograph without a sense of the full texture of a composition. At times, Macdonald had managed to persuade the Canadian Broadcasting Corporation to play the work on the radio well in advance of the ballet. Then one can get a good recording. The problems that arise with the musicians' unions have to be resolved so that it becomes feasible for choreographers to acquire a good working tape.

There was some confusion of issues and vigorous argument when the subject turned from music to the restaging of the classics. A questioner wanted to know what role the choreographer of today had in retaining the classics. The ballets that have been passed down to us are not necessarily even in quality. If changes are to be made, who is to be the arbiter of taste? How much do we keep and how much do we edit?

As Rudi van Dantzig pointed out, we are already in a position where it has become hard to be sure what is "authentic." For him, the very idea of touching the classics is full of dangers. Even the Russians have now fiddled around with some of the great Tchaikovsky-Petipa ballets. Mr. van Dantzig was opposed to this.

The question, however, remains. In staging a classic, there will be points of uncertainty, even when one is trying to stay true to the original. What then?

When the Sadler's Wells Ballet, later to become the Royal Ballet, had produced *The Sleeping Beauty* to reopen the Royal Opera House after World War II, they had been able to call on the services of Nicholas Sergeyev who had left Russia after the revolution with the Stepanov notation of many Maryinsky Theatre productions. When the Sadler's Wells had taken the Sergeyev staging of *The Sleeping Beauty* to Russia a moving incident occurred. Dame Ninette and Sir Frederick Ashton were strolling through the theatre when an elderly gentleman came up and simply said, "Petipa and Tchaikovsky should both have been here tonight!"

But, in the absence of reliable notation, the panelists saw it as the responsibility of the artistic director to make sure that any adjustments that must be done to a classic are made in keeping with the style of the work. The problems might never be fully resolved, but if the purity of the classics is to be preserved at all, no trouble can be considered too great in staging them.

Ming Cho Lee unintentionally opened Pandora's Box by suggesting that the classics could be given many kinds of modern interpretations. He drew analogies with contemporary stagings of Shakespeare's plays and Wagner's operas, only to be shot down by the purists.

For them, his analogy did not work. Interpretation in drama is very different from interpretation in ballet. Once steps are changed it is simply a different ballet. This has to necessarily occur from time to time. To do it on a grand scale might risk losing the original, especially when ballet, unlike music and drama, cannot be adequately recorded in all its dimensions.

Despite opposition, Ming Cho Lee still saw room for reinterpretation. "There is absolutely no harm in doing a socialist *Giselle* or even a women's lib *Giselle*." As a compromise he suggested having both a traditional and a modern version of historic works in the repertoire.

Another member of the audience wanted to know how the three panelists managed to combine direction of a company with their own choreography. Brian Macdonald gave up the artistic direction of Les Grands Ballets Canadiens early in 1978, but at the time of the conference still had to apportion his time and energy between two very demanding jobs. On balance, it was an impossible situation in which something was bound to suffer. The modern director has so many responsibilities, not all of them strictly artistic, that it leaves his creative energies drained.

Robert Joffrey, who has largely given up choreographing, and Rudi van Dantzig both described how creative it can be to hold a director's responsibilities. The overall style of a company, the selection of the dancers, the choice of a repertory, everything that is ultimately seen on stage and most of what happens off it, falls to the director.

Despite the hazards, there can also be advantages to directing a company *and* choreographing. In a sense, a choreographer may feel impelled to direct a company for self-protection. Some choreographers cannot find it in themselves to allow their work to be performed beyond their immediate supervision. Brian Macdonald recalled an occasion that illustrated how the situation could work to the choreographer's advantage.

"In 1975 I did a ballet for the Paris Opera. It was just a superb flop. The booing lasted for about 25 minutes. But I knew there was good work in there and I was determined. I came back to Canada and set it on my own company with corrections. It turned out to be one of the best things I've done in a long time. Being director, I could program it. Had I not been, it would have been hard to get another opportunity to set a ballet already labelled a flop by the people in Paris."

In their presentations, both Rudi van Dantzig and Brian Macdonald had, if not directly, at least by implication, touched on matters of ideology, on matters of social and nationalistic concern. A final question from the audience posed an important issue. Can a choreographer keep a safeguard on himself so that his work will not become mere dogma, simply propaganda? Can he keep his objectivity and not lose the sense that he is creating a work of art? "Art by committee never really works."

The question, as Rudi van Dantzig showed, did not make clear what is meant by "propaganda." Above all, sincerity is the most important element in choreography. "I saw a film of the Chinese where the women had guns on stage. It upset me so greatly I walked out—and I do not do that sort of thing normally. But take something like Kurt Jooss' *The Green Table*. It is a certain form of propaganda. It survives because it takes a human form and was created from great belief, from a sense of the necessity to express true feeling. If it had been simply propaganda it would have folded long ago. It stays with us because it came out of Jooss' sincerity."

CONTRIBUTORS'
BIOGRAPHIES

Louis Applebaum

Louis Applebaum is a Canadian composer, conductor and administrator. After attending the University of Toronto (1936-40), scholarships enabled him to study in New York with Roy Harris and Bernard Wagenaar. On returning to Canada in 1941, he became Staff Composer and, later, Music Director of the National Film Board of Canada. Further film work followed in New York and Hollywood—including the score for *The Story of GI Joe*, nominated for an Academy Award in 1947.

In 1955, Mr. Applebaum became Music Director of the Shakespearean Festival, Stratford, Ontario. He inaugurated a music festival as part of the program, and was responsible for an International Conference of Composers at Stratford in 1960. He has composed incidental scores for over 30 Festival productions, and conducted many Festival opera and operetta presentations.

After two years as music consultant to CBC-TV (1960-61), Mr. Applebaum became increasingly more involved in arts administrative activities, without ever giving up composition. He has served such bodies as the Canada Council, The National Arts Centre, and The Composers, Authors and Publishers Association of Canada. In 1971, he was appointed Executive Director of the Province of Ontario Council for the Arts.

The greater part of Mr. Applebaum's extensive musical output has been for stage, television, radio, ballet and film. Some of these scores were later arranged for concert performance, including the ballet music, *Barbara Allen*, composed for the National Ballet of Canada.

Sir Frederick Ashton

Sir Frederick Ashton is generally considered to be one of the greatest choreographers the ballet has produced. His creative versatility and gift for adapting historical ballets has earned him a world-wide reputation for faultless taste, sensitivity and economy of means.

Born in Ecuador, Sir Frederick Ashton saw Pavlova dance in 1913 during a South American tour. From then on, he knew his vocation was the ballet.

Moving to England in 1919, he studied with Massine and Rambert. His first ballet, *A Tragedy of Fashion*, appeared in 1926. He danced in various companies until becoming chief choreographer of the Vic-Wells Ballet in 1935. His career remained within this company as it became the Sadler's Wells Ballet and eventually, in 1956, the Royal Ballet. He was appointed associate director in 1952 and was director from 1963 to 1970. He continues to be closely associated with the company. Indeed, the Royal Ballet's stylistic identity is in large measure the result of his influence.

During his career, Sir Frederick Ashton has worked as a guest choreographer with many leading companies and his ballets are performed by countless companies around the world. The National Ballet of Canada performs *La fille mal gardée* and several other of Ashton's ballets.

He created many ballets for Margot Fonteyn, in whose remarkable artistry he found inspiration, and for Alexander Grant, whose unmatched gifts as a demi-caractère were exploited by Ashton in a succession of memorable roles.

Among Sir Frederick Ashton's most celebrated ballets have been: *Façade* (1931), *Les Rendezvous* (1933), *Apparitions* (1936), *Les Patineurs* (1937), *A Wedding Bouquet* (1937). *Symphonic Variations* (1946), *Cinderella* (1948), *Daphnis and Chlöe* (1950), *Romeo and Juliet* (1955), *Ondine* (1958), *La fille mal gardée* (1960), *The Two Pigeons* (1961), *Marguerite and Armand* (1963), *The Dream* (1964), *Monotones* (1965-6), *Enigma Variations* (1968) and *A Month in the Country* (1976).

Sir Frederick Ashton has been honoured in many countries for his enormous contribution to the ballet. He holds Britain's two most distinguished honours, the Order of Merit and the Companion of Honour, and was knighted in 1962.

Clive Barnes

Clive Barnes, a Londoner by birth, is one of the English-speaking world's most famous dance and drama critics.

His critical career began while he was still an undergraduate at Oxford. From 1952-1961 Clive Barnes used the relative security of an administrative job in the London County Council as the base for the more precarious existence of a freelance journalist. He wrote extensively on music, the dance, theatre, films and television for *The New Statesman, The Spectator,* and the *Daily Express* as well as *Dance and Dancers* magazine (of which he became an Associate Editor in 1950), and the *New York Times.* From 1961-1965 he was chief dance critic of *The Times* of London and Executive Editor of *Dance and Dancers, Music and Musicians* and *Plays and Players.* He has also written or contributed to a number of books.

In 1965 he joined the *New York Times* as dance critic, adding the drama beat from 1967. He moved to the *New York Post* in November 1977 where he continues to write about dance and drama.

Peter Brinson

Peter Brinson's distinguished career in dance has taken him to many parts of the world as a lecturer and consultant. He is the author of many books, television programs and ballet plays about various aspects of dance. He was the founding director of the Royal Ballet's "Ballet For All" company, which has had a major role in building and educating an audience for dance in Britain.

Peter Brinson was a visiting lecturer and adjunct professor in the Department of Dance at York University, Ontario, (1970-1975), and since 1972 has been director of the United Kingdom and Commonwealth Branch of the Calouste Gulbenkian Foundation, whose Dance Program he also chairs.

Norman Campbell

Norman Campbell is among Canada's most distinguished and successful television producers and directors. He was born in California but was reared and educated in Vancouver where he began his broadcasting career as a radio producer in the late forties.

In 1952, he moved to Toronto and television. His work for the CBC has covered a broad range of music, comedy and variety programs but his first love has always been the televising of ballet. Since 1956, when he produced the first of a number of televised adaptations of *Swan Lake*, Norman Campbell has directed 15 major television ballets, most of them with the National Ballet of Canada. Two of these, *Cinderella* (1970) and *The Sleeping Beauty* (1973), won Emmy Awards. His production of *Romeo and Juliet* won the Prix René Barthelmy in 1965. His most recent work with the National Ballet was a production of Frederick Ashton's *La fille mal gardée*, broadcast in January, 1979.

Norman Campbell has also made frequent trips abroad on commission to direct both for film and television. His film, *Ballerina*, made for Walt Disney in 1964 and using the dancers of the Royal Danish Ballet, is still seen today.

Ludmilla Chiriaeff

Ludmilla Chiriaeff is Founder and Director of Les Grands Ballets Canadiens, a company with a repertoire both classical and contemporary, a position which emerged in 1958 from her activity as a choreographer for CBC-TV (Montreal) during the early fifties.

Born in Riga, Latvia, Madame Chiriaeff studied as a child with Alexandra Nicolaieva and, while a member of Colonel de Basil's Ballets Russes, had the opportunity to work with Leonide Massine, David Lichine and Michel Fokine, who, in particular, encouraged her work as a teacher and choreographer.

Before the Second World War she worked at the Berlin Opera Ballet and, in 1945, became première danseuse and choreographer at the Municipal Theatre of Lausanne and subsequently at the Kursaal Theatre of Geneva. Shortly afterward she founded her first dance company, Le Ballet des Arts de Genève. In 1952, however, she emigrated to Canada.

Apart from establishing a firm place in the dance world for her own company, Ludmilla Chiriaeff's work as a teacher has made an important contribution to the development of ballet in French Canada.

In 1975, l'École Supérieure, in cooperation with the Quebec Ministry of Education and the St. Croix School Commission, initiated a unique professional dance program that permitted, for the first time, fully professional ballet training within the curriculum of a regular high school.

Madame Chiriaeff received the Order of Canada in 1969.

Michael Crabb

Michael Crabb is a writer, editor, teacher and broadcaster. He emigrated from England to Canada in 1969 and began writing about dance while a graduate student and teaching assistant at McMaster University in Hamilton, Ontario. In 1974, he became Dance Editor of *Performing Arts in Canada*, a national quarterly magazine and, in 1977, succeeded Susan Cohen as Editor of *Dance in Canada* magazine.

He has written for many publications in North America and England, and produced the text for Andrew Oxenham's collection of photographs, *Dance Today in Canada* (Toronto, Simon and Pierre, 1977).

Michael Crabb is also Head of the History Department at Appleby College, Oakville, Ontario.

George Crum

George Crum has been Musical Director and Conductor of the National Ballet of Canada since its inception in 1951, winning repeated accolades for his sensitivity toward and respect for the integrity of music in dance and ballet. He has also acquired a substantial reputation as an arranger of ballet scores.

Before joining the National Ballet, George Crum had been a piano soloist and had been deeply involved with operatic music. He conducted *Faust* for the Royal Conservatory Opera (later to become the Canadian Opera Company) at the age of 22.

Although the growing activity of the National Ballet restricted his opportunities for other musical engagements, Mr. Crum continued to coach singers and conduct for opera.

Margaret Dale

Margaret Dale is a film-maker and television producer now working in dance and education. She was soloist in the Sadler's Wells Ballet (now the Royal Ballet) from 1937-1954, when she joined the British Broadcasting Corporation. She has made over 100 television programs, including studio productions of works of the Royal Ballet and other leading companies, as well as films—on historical and contemporary subjects.

Margaret Dale was Chairperson of the Department of Dance at York University, Ontario from 1976-1977.

She received an award for ballet production from the Society of Film and Television Arts in November, 1963.

Rudi van Dantzig

Rudi van Dantzig has been Artistic Director of the Dutch National Ballet (whose staff he joined in 1965) since 1971. Before that he had studied and danced with Sonia Gaskell for whom he produced his first ballet, *Nachteiland* (Night Island).

It is as a choreographer that Mr. van Dantzig is best known around the world. His many ballets, created in a dance language full of symbolism, have focused on the psychological travails of the individual, on themes of good and evil, love and death. His works may be seen in the repertory of many companies around the world including the Ballet Rambert, the Royal Danish Ballet, American Ballet Theatre, the National Ballet of Canada and several other companies.

Lukas Foss

Lukas Foss is one of America's leading musical personalities—as a composer, conductor, teacher and performer. The recipient of numerous prizes, awards and commissions, his contribution to the cause of American music won him the Ditson Conductor's Award of Columbia University in 1974. In 1978 he received the Mayor of New York's Award for a Special Contribution to the Arts.

As a teacher, Mr. Foss served on the staff of the Berkshire Music Center, where he had earlier studied, and succeeded Arnold Schoenberg as Professor of Composition at the University of California, Los Angeles, where he remained for ten years before accepting the musical directorship of the Buffalo Philharmonic (1963-1970).

His championship of musical innovation in performance and composition made Buffalo the focal point of international attention.

For several years he was conductor and musical advisor of the Jerusalem Symphony (until 1977) as well as the Brooklyn Philharmonia, where he remains as director and conductor.

Mr. Foss has appeared as guest conductor with many of the world's leading orchestras and conducted the first performance of Xenakis' score for Roland Petit's *Kraanerg*, which the National Ballet of Canada presented for the inauguration of the National Arts Centre in Ottawa (1969).

Harry Freedman

Harry Freedman was brought to Canada from his native Poland at the age of three by his family, who settled first in Medicine Hat and then Winnipeg.

His first artistic interest was painting and he did not begin his musical studies until he was 18. After WWII service in the air force, he moved to Toronto, studied at the Royal Conservatory and, on scholarship, at Tanglewood with Olivier Messiaen and Aaron Copland.

From 1949-1970 he played English horn in the Toronto Symphony, while beginning to compose. His work has been performed internationally and his scores for radio, television, film and stage have brought Harry Freedman wide recognition. He has written four ballet scores for Brian Macdonald, *Rose Latulippe* (in 1966, the first full-length ballet to be produced in North America). *Five Over Thirteen* (1969), *The Shining People of Leonard Cohen* (1970) and *Romeo and Juliet* (1973).

Mr. Freedman has always been very interested in educational music and has produced, with support from the Canada Council, an extensive series of graded pieces for high school players employing musical idioms and techniques of the 20th century.

Alexander Grant

Alexander Grant has, since 1976, been Artistic Director of the National Ballet of Canada, the sequel to a 30-year career as one of the Royal Ballet's greatest and best-loved dancers.

A demi-caractère of international fame, he began life in New Zealand, emigrating to England in 1946 to study at the Sadler's Wells Ballet School. Within six months he had joined the company and was soon featured as the Dandy in Leonide Massine's revival of *The Three-Cornered Hat* and later as the Barber in *Mam'Zelle Angot*. But it was in the ballets of Frederick Ashton that Alexander Grant's talent found its fullest expression. Among the first of these Ashton roles was the Jester in *Cinderella* (1948)—the last, in 1976, was as the husband, Yslaev, in *A Month in the Country*. Perhaps he will best be remembered as Alain in *La fille mal gardée* and as Bottom in *The Dream*.

During his last five years in London, Alexander Grant also directed "Ballet For All"—a small touring offshoot of the Royal Ballet—for whom he produced a number of programs.

In 1965 he was named Commander of the Order of the British Empire for his service to ballet.

Robert Joffrey

Robert Joffrey ranks among the leaders of ballet in America, having founded, sustained and lead to international distinction his own company (against severe odds and setbacks), since 1956.

Although he finds little opportunity nowadays to choreograph, Robert Joffrey has created numerous ballets including *Pas de Déesses* (1954), *Gamelan* (1962) and *Remembrances* (1973).

Apart from the time-consuming task of running a ballet company, Mr. Joffrey still teaches and lectures. His major contribution to ballet has been widely acclaimed. He has received both the Dance Magazine Award (1963) and the Capezio Award (1974).

Ming Cho Lee

Ming Cho Lee moved from his native China in 1949 to study in the United States, where he later settled. He has become one of America's foremost designers for the stage. From 1962-1973 he was Principal Designer of the New York Shakespeare Festival and has designed many productions for Broadway shows, regional theatre companies and for dance. In 1974 he designed the set for the National Ballet of Canada's production of Norbert Vesak's *Whispers of Darkness* and has worked extensively in the United States for such renowned choreographers as José Limon, Martha Graham, Alvin Ailey, Gerald Arpino and Anthony Tudor, whose most recent ballet he designed in 1978.

William Littler

William Littler was born in Vancouver, where he studied piano and musical theory and graduated from the University of British Columbia. At the age of 22, he became music and dance critic of the *Vancouver Sun* but in 1966 moved east to join the staff of the *Toronto Star* as music critic. Upon the death of Nathan Cohen in 1971, he added dance to his existing responsibilities in music.

A frequent broadcaster and contributor to journals in music and dance,

William Littler is also adjunct associate professor in the Faculty of Fine Arts at York University, Toronto, where he teaches courses in theatre history and dance criticism.

He is Vice-President of the Music Critics Association and chaired the first North American Dance Critics Conference in New York (1974), from which emerged the Dance Critics Association. He became its founding chairman. He also directed the first Critics Institute in Canadian Music in Toronto, Ottawa and Montreal in 1975 and headed an Interdisciplinary Critics Workshop at York University in 1978.

Brian Macdonald

Brian Macdonald is Canada's most eminent choreographer. His work has appeared in the repertoire of many companies around the world including, among others, the National Ballet of Canada, The Royal Winnipeg Ballet, the Royal Swedish Ballet, London Festival Ballet, Joffrey Ballet, Dutch National Ballet, National Ballet of Cuba and Les Grands Ballets Canadiens, of which he was Artistic Director from 1974 to 1978 and where he remains as Resident Choreographer. He has also directed the Royal Swedish Ballet and Harkness Ballet.

A Montrealer by birth, Brian Macdonald began his career, after graduation from McGill University, as a music critic but quickly found his true vocation as a choreographer and teacher.

He received the Gold Star for choreography in the Paris International Dance Festival of 1964, and in 1967 was awarded the Order of Canada.

John Percival

John Percival, like his colleague Clive Barnes, is a Londoner and a former student of St. Catherine's College, Oxford. It was there he began to write about ballet; he has been on the staff of *Dance and Dancers* since its earliest issues in 1950. He succeeded Mr. Barnes at the *Times* in 1965 and is London correspondent of *Dance Magazine* and the German annual *Ballet*.

John Percival has produced several books, of which *Nureyev—Aspects of the Dancer* is his most recent.

Timothy Porteous

Timothy Porteous became Associate Director of the Canada Council in 1973 after an earlier career in the law and the civil service—as Executive Assistant to the Prime Minister.

Born in Montreal and a graduate of McGill University, he also studied in Paris. His name became well known in 1957 as co-author of a highly successful Canadian musical satire, *My Fur Lady*.

His interest in the performing arts has led him to be associated in various capacities with the National Theatre School, Theatre Canada and the Montreal Symphony Orchestra.

Arnold Spohr

Arnold Spohr has been Artistic Director of the Royal Winnipeg Ballet for 20 years, before that appearing as a dancer (1947-1954) and working as a choreographer.

He has led his company on numerous foreign tours—to South America, Australia, Israel, Russia, Czechoslovakia, England, Italy and France—and has earned wide respect as a sensitive director, coach and teacher.

Born in Saskatchewan, he trained as a pianist before entering the ballet. His devotion both to his own company and to the cause of ballet in Canada has earned Arnold Spohr many awards including an honorary doctorate from the University of Manitoba and the Order of Canada.

Veronica Tennant

Veronica Tennant was thrust into stardom while still in her teens when, fresh from the National Ballet School, she made her debut with the National Ballet of Canada in the title role of John Cranko's *Romeo and Juliet*, seen a year later, in 1966, by a vast audience in an award-winning televised version.

A dramatic ballerina of formidable intensity, Veronica Tennant has won acclaim as much for her superb technique and sensitive phrasing as for the intelligence and conviction of her interpretations of the great classical roles.

Veronica Tennant danced in both CBC-TV productions that won Emmy Awards, *Cinderella* (1970) and *The Sleeping Beauty* (1973).

She has made frequent guest appearances and has been partnered by some of the foremost classical dancers of our age, among them Rudolf Nureyev, Mikhail Baryshnikov, Edward Villella, Fernando Bujones, Ivan Nagy and Stephen Jefferies.

In the midst of so much performing she has found time to sit on the board of the Ontario Arts Council, to write a children's novel and to have a child.

In 1975 she was invested with the Order of Canada.

Vincent Tovell

Vincent Tovell has for many years been a leading figure in the cultural life of Canada. During a long career in broadcasting he has been announcer, actor, interviewer, writer and producer. He joined the staff of the CBC in 1953 and is today an Executive Producer for television.

His most memorable work in recent years has been the 10 hour-long films for the series *Images of Canada* and a two-part documentary drama, *The Masseys: Chronicles of a Canadian Family*.

Vincent Tovell's personal interests in painting, sculpture and music, together with his professional activity in theatre, film, teaching and broadcasting have led him into close involvement with many arts organizations, principally among them, the Art Gallery of Ontario, the National Ballet School of Canada and the Canadian Conference of the Arts. From 1966-1970 he was first chairman of the Canada Council's Arts Advisory Panel.

Dame Ninette de Valois

Dame Ninette de Valois is one of the most important figures of 20th century ballet, founder of the Royal Ballet, and a legend in her own lifetime.

Irish by birth, Dame Ninette de Valois studied with several teachers, including the great Enrico Cecchetti. She began dancing professionally in 1914, becoming a member of the Diaghilev Ballet in 1923. In 1926 she left to found her own school from which she hoped a British ballet company might one day emerge. Groups of her students began performing at the Old Vic in London, then directed by Lilian Baylis, and when, in 1931, the Sadler's Wells Theatre was reopened she moved her school into the theatre and founded a small company.

From these early beginnings, about which Dame Ninette de Valois has written extensively, emerged a company that has since become renowned the world over. Although she retired as director of the Royal Ballet in 1961, she continues to be closely involved with the company she founded and for which she created many ballets, most notably *Job* (1931) and *The Rake's Progress* (1935).

Internationally acclaimed for her services to the ballet and the recipient of many awards, she became a Dame Commander of the Order of the British Empire in 1951, although she continued to be known as she is to this day, both affectionately and fearfully, as "Madame."

SUGGESTIONS
for FURTHER READING

Barnes, Clive. *Inside American Ballet Theatre.* (New York: Hawthorn Books, 1977)

Beaumont, Cyril William. *The Diaghilev Ballet in London.* (London: A. and C. Black, 1951)

Bell, Ken (photographs) and Celia Franca (A Memoir). *The National Ballet of Canada: A Celebration.* (Toronto: University of Toronto Press, 1978)

Bland, Alexander. *A History of Ballet and Dance in the Western World.* (New York: Praeger, 1976)

Brinson, Peter. "The Development of Professional Training for Classical Ballet in Canada." *Canada Council Report*, 1974

Clarke, Mary and David Vaughan, eds. *The Encyclopedia of Dance and Ballet.* (Toronto: Copp Clark, 1977)

Cohen, Selma Jean (editor, with commentary). *Dance as a Theatre Art. Source Readings in Dance History From 1581 to the Present.* (New York: Dodd, Mead and Company, 1974)

Coton, A.V. *Writings on Dance, 1938-68; selected by Katherine Sorley Walker and Lilian Haddakin.* (London: Dance Books, 1975)

Denby, Edwin. Introduction by B.H. Haggin. *Looking At Dance.* (New York: Horizon, 1968)

De Valois, Ninette. *Step By Step: The Formation of an Establishment.* (London: W.H. Allen, 1977)

Franks, A.H. *Ballet For Film and Television.* (London: Pitman, 1950)
        . *Twentieth Century Ballet.* (London: Burke, 1954)

Haskell, Arnold Lionel. *Diaghilev, His Artistic and Private Life.* (New York: Simon and Schuster, 1935)

Kersley, Leo and Janet Sinclair. *A Dictionary of Ballet Terms.* (New York: Pitman, 1964, new edition, 1973)

Kirstein, Lincoln. *Dance: A Short History of Classical Theatrical Dancing.* (New York: Putnam, 1935)
. *Movement and Metaphor: Four Centuries of Ballet.* (New York: Praeger, 1970)

Koegler, Horst. *The Concise Oxford Dictionary of Ballet.* (Toronto: Oxford University Press, 1977)

Lifar, Serge. *Serge Diaghilev, His Life, His Work, His Legend: An Intimate Biography.* (New York: Putnam, 1940)

Lorrain, Roland. *Les Grands Ballets Canadiens.* (Montreal: Editions du Jour, 1973). Published in French.

Martin, John. *Introduction to the Dance.* (New York: Dance Horizons, 1965)

Monahan, James. *The Nature of Ballet: A Critic's Reflections.* (Toronto: Copp Clark, 1976)

Oxenham, Andrew (photographs) with Michael Crabb (text). *Dance Today in Canada*. (Toronto: Simon and Pierre, 1977)

Percival, John. *Nureyev—Aspects of the Dancer*. (Toronto: Clark Irwin, 1975)
        . *The World of Diaghilev*. (London: Studio Vista, 1971)

Searle, Humphrey. *Ballet Music*. (New York: Dover, 1958). Revised 1973

Stevens, Franklin. *Dance as Life: A Season With American Ballet Theatre*. (Don Mills: Fitzhenry and Whiteside, 1976)

Taper, Bernard. *Balanchine: A Biography*. (New York: Collier Macmillan, 1960). Revised and updated 1974

Terry, Walter. *The Dance in America*. (New York: Harper and Row, 1956). Revised 1971

Varley, Gloria (text) and Peter Varley (photographs). *To Be A Dancer: Canada's National Ballet School*. (Toronto: Peter Martin Associates, 1971)

Vaughan, David. *Frederick Ashton and His Ballets.* (Toronto: Thomas Nelson and Sons, 1977)

Whittaker, Herbert. *Canada's National Ballet.* (Toronto: McClelland and Stewart, 1967)

Wyman, Max. *The Royal Winnipeg Ballet: The First Forty Years.* (Toronto: Doubleday, 1978)

INDEX